THE
ROCKING-HORSE
MAKER

THE
ROCKING-
HORSE
MAKER

Nine easy-to-follow projects

Anthony Dew

David & Charles

For my Mother and Father

A DAVID & CHARLES BOOK

First published 1993

A catalogue record for this book is available from the British Library

ISBN 0 7153 0086 5

Designed and typeset by Les Dominey Design Company
on an Apple Macintosh System
and printed in Italy by New Interlitho SpA
for David & Charles
Brunel House Newton Abbot Devon

AUTHOR'S NOTE

You don't have to be a highly skilled woodworker to make a good rocking-horse. It is the kind of project which invariably succeeds, given an enthusiastic and persistent approach.

This book caters for all abilities and the simpler designs will certainly be within the scope of anyone with a basic tool kit and modest skills. The clear and thorough descriptions and wealth of pictures are aimed at ensuring that when you start one of the projects, you *will* succeed. Even experienced wood-workers will find plenty of opportunity for exercising their skills, especially with the more ambitious projects; no one has yet made the perfect rocking-horse.

The techniques described are for the most part 'traditional', employing hand-carving tools such as the mallet and gouge (though we do recommend modern glues, paints, electric drills etc). But the book is not a nostalgic wallow in out-dated craft skills. It is for people today who still recognise the immense value of hand-craft, both in the appreciation and, more importantly, in the doing. Few things compare with the sense of real personal achievement which derives from simply making something – and more so when you make something which is both beautiful and which you know will give a great deal of pleasure to others.
You never know, rocking-horse making may take over *your* life!

Anthony Dew,
Fangfoss, York
July 1993

CONTENTS

INTRODUCTION

When I first became interested in making rocking-horses, many years ago now, it was almost a dead craft. The last of the big toy manufacturers to make carved wooden rocking-horses had ceased production during World War II and had never resumed. This was not surprising: making carved wooden rocking-horses is a labour- and skill-intensive business, not suited to the mass-production requirements of modern industry. Some toy manufacturers did, and do, continue to make rocking-horses, but they tend to be smaller and simpler designs, occasionally wooden, more often metal or plastic, or fur-fabric covered. One company started to produce Victorian-style rocking-horses in the early 1970s, made from moulded fibreglass. But carved wooden rocking-horse making was all but extinct.

Back then we frequently heard the comment, 'Aren't they lovely, you just don't see real rocking-horses any more.' We do not hear that remark much now, because there has been a great revival of interest in handcrafts in general, and rocking-horse making in particular, and there are now a surprising number of small businesses specialising in the making and restoration of traditional rocking-horses. Proper rocking-horses are no longer as rare as their proverbial manure, and I find this most gratifying. The surprising response to my first book (*Making Rocking Horses*, published by David & Charles in 1984) showed that there was a considerable interest in this fascinating craft, and we have received many letters from enthusiasts and aspiring makers all over the world.

What we were trying to do at the outset was to make a proper-looking rocking-horse (like Granny used to ride) which would be hand-carved and finished, with real leather tack, flowing mane and tail and glinting glass eyes that would promise any child an exciting ride. My rocking-horse designs are based on traditional styles, but are in a continuous state of change, development and improvement. Some are quite simple and easy to make, others inevitably more involved. This book contains the results of our efforts over the last few years. There are projects here to suit all abilities, starting with simple hobby-horses (Chapter 1), and a

toddler's rocking-horse (Chapter 3) which can be successfully accomplished even by people who have only dabbled in woodwork. Carved-head options are given for those who have not done any carving before, but who would like to try. The Swinger horse in Chapter 4 has a proper swing-iron rocking action but the horse is easy to make since it involves no carving, while the Little Red Rocker (Chapter 5) has some interesting carved elements, though it is still relatively easy to make.

Designs for 'real' fully carved traditional-style rocking-horses are described in Chapters 6, 8 and 9, while Chapter 13 features a design for a carousel-style horse and is presented as a challenge for more ambitious woodcarvers. None of the designs involves complicated joints, and the construction method for each project has been kept as straightforward as practicable. A fairly modest tool kit is all that is needed to make the projects in this book, and most woodworkers will already have the majority of the basic tools required. Although the carving obviously demands some specialised carving gouges and so on (see Chapter 2), it should not be necessary to spend a lot of money on tools and equipment in order to make any of these projects. Indeed, to make the miniature rocking-horse in Chapter 12, for example, you need little more than a fretsaw and a sharp knife.

A rocking-horse is a wonderful vehicle for a child's imagination, and he occupies a special place among playthings. His size, 'personality' and solidity set him apart from smaller toys. A child will develop a much more intimate relationship with a rocking-horse than with the large, impersonal playground swings and see-saws. A rocking-horse can be a very real friend to a lonely child and he possesses, for the younger child, many of the qualities of a real horse with none of the drawbacks. He never needs feeding or exercising on frosty winter mornings, he can look after himself and doesn't resent occasional neglect. He never needs to be mucked out. And he is absolutely tireless; always ready to take the child rider on the most exciting yet secure imaginative gallops.

To make a fully carved rocking-horse can be a rather challenging prospect, and we are often asked, 'Do you think I can do it?'. Well, we cannot answer that question, except to say that many people have made one, even those with limited woodworking experience, and made a splendid job of it. We are frequently sent enthusiastic letters – accompanied by photographs of the finished product – from people who have used our plans to make rocking-horses. We are always delighted to receive these, and it is fascinating to see the varied results that arise, even when starting from the same basic plan, because each horse is unique and each maker gives something of his or her self to the project.

A wooden rocking-horse is much more than just a toy of the moment, and, in spite of the plethora of high-tech electronic games now in vogue, it remains a firm favourite. He will outlast several generations of young riders. He will become a family heirloom and be passed down to new generations who will always greet him with pleasure. And when, after many years of use, his mane and tail and saddle become tattered, his paintwork chipped and cracked, and his mechanical parts worn and rickety, he can be repaired and refurbished and given a whole new lease of life. Chapter 14 looks at some of the problems of restoring old rocking-horses.

I hope that this book will encourage many more people to discover the fascination of rocking-horse making. Do read all the instructions thoroughly so that you have a clear understanding of what each project entails. To make a rocking-horse and to see it enjoyed by your children and grandchildren is a source of a very special sense of achievement and satisfaction.

Nine year-old-rider on the Large rocking-horse described in chapter 9

Fine old Victorian rocking-horse (after restoration by the author)

CHAPTER 1
HISTORY AND HOBBY-HORSES

When you hear a baby crying the usual reaction is to pick it up and cradle it in your arms, making soothing noises as you gently rock the child. This generally has the desired effect and the baby's crying subsides. The reason may be partly because of the warmth and comforting effect of the cuddle and the soft cooing noises, but undoubtedly the rocking motion has a soothing effect. There has in fact been some research conducted into the efficaciousness of rocking. The result of this study showed that unless it is actually distressed by pain, fear or discomfort, rocking is the almost-infallible way to quiet a crying baby. I have a feeling that even without or before the benefit of scientific findings any mother would broadly agree with this. Hence rocking cradles, which have been used at least since medieval times and probably for much longer.

Rocking is not only good for settling crying babies. It has a similar effect on children of all ages, who not infrequently rock themselves back and forth if sad or unhappy, or just bored. Mentally disturbed people do it, as do perfectly sane adults, in rocking-chairs. It is a physical form of the repeated mantra of meditators; a panacea; a way to soothe and ease the mind. As far as rocking-horses are concerned, it is fun too.

ORIGINS OF THE ROCKING-HORSE

Horses (real ones) have been a vital component of the development of almost every civilisation; and since almost every adult concern is imitated in appropriate playthings for children, it is not surprising that toy horses have been made from earliest times. Of course, children's toys are frequently roughly used: if a real horse is made to gallop across muddy fields, a toy horse will be made to do the same; so they become broken, worn and discarded. Also, they are often made from perishable materials, and not many really old toy horses survive to the present day. Nevertheless, a few have done so, made from clay, terracotta and even wood, that date back several thousands of years.

Many of these ancient model horses have been excavated from burial sites, and they may have been made as burial artefacts rather than as children's playthings. The lifesize model horses found in China with the terracotta army, for example, were clearly not intended as toys. With a few notable exceptions such as these, ancient toy horses are mostly quite small, certainly too small to be ridden, though sometimes they have wheels, like pull-along toys. But if small model horses were made as burial artefacts, I am certain that they were also made as children's toys. What child who saw one of these little horses could resist wanting to play with it? And what artisan could resist making one or two for his children's amusement or education?

The simplest form of toy horse, which also dates from at least medieval times, is the hobby-horse. At its most basic the hobby-horse is a representation of a horse's head, mounted on a stick. Children love a toy with which they can become actively involved and control. Astride the hobby-horse, they can gallop about crying 'Whoa!' and 'Gee-up!'. I have seen children using a broom as a hobby-horse, the broom head serving as a substitute for the horse's head. Purpose-made hobby-horses sometimes have heads that are only crudely or simply fashioned, or they may be quite finely shaped and detailed; often there is a wheel at the lower end of the stick. They can be quite elaborate. English Morris dancers sometimes employ a type of hobby-horse with an almost-lifesize head and cane framework strapped on to the rider, around which is draped a long cloth that conceals the rider's legs. It is always the 'rider's' legs that do the galloping.

The history of the rocking-horse proper starts in the early seventeenth century, when some anonymous person realised that it was possible to make a toy horse big enough for children to actually climb upon and ride. Although such a wooden toy was bound to be heavy, it could be made to move by mounting it upon curved rockers. This really was rather a clever idea, and it worked. On the earliest rocking-horses the rockers were made from two almost-semicircular slabs of solid timber, arranged side by side but converging towards the top where a narrow plank formed the seat. On this was fixed a carving of a horse's head and neck, and a seatback. They also usually had a foot-rest strategically placed at either side. All made from solid timber, they were indeed heavy. But given the right balance and arc of curvature of the rockers, it was quite possible for even a small child to make them rock. A very effective rocking action it was, too. The child was in complete control and could vary the rocking at will, from a soothing and gentle to-and-fro to an exciting 'gallop'.

With curved rockers, especially if they are made too short, there is a danger that an enthusiastic rider could overturn the horse. This was prevented by cutting stops into the rockers at both ends. These restrict the rocking action slightly — the horse can be rocked as far as the stops but no further — but do make it a lot safer. A solid wooden rocking-horse overturning on its rider could obviously be injurious. Not that safety seems to have been a very big factor in the early design of these toys. They were frequently regarded not only as amusements, but as an effective apparatus for training young riders for the saddle. An element of danger was permissible, even welcomed.

Some of these early slab-sided rocking-horses had the shape of the body and the legs of the horse painted, or even carved, on the rocker sides. But it was not long before it was realised (again by some anonymous but rather clever person) that a much more attractive and realistic appearance could be achieved by making the rockers out of long and thin bow-shaped arcs of timber and mounting on them a fully carved

horse. This gave rise to the characteristic and now-traditional rocking-horse of the eighteenth and nineteenth centuries, often referred to as mounted on 'Georgian' bows. Apart from being splendid playthings, these can be beautifully carved and finished. Quite a few remain in existence in museums and collections, but only rarely in their original condition.

The inventive Victorians produced many patents and designs which attempted to improve upon the bow rocker. Some employing springs or levers enjoyed limited commercial success, but most were too complicated or impractical to be taken up, and, one suspects, never left the drawing board. But a patent filed by P. W. Marqua of Cincinnati, USA, in 1878 and two years later in Britain, proved to be the one that had all the characteristics of a successful design. It was simple, easy to make and fit, effective and relatively safe in use. This was the swing-iron stand, and it became so successful that it virtually superseded the old bow-rocker style, particularly for larger horses. It is much the commonest form of rocking mechanism in use today, except for small toddler-size horses where curved rockers remain the favourite.

There is a tremendous variety of styles, construction methods and finishes used on wooden rocking-horses, whether they are made for mounting on bow rockers or swing-iron stands. They range from simple board constructions, with little or no carving or fancy decoration, to beautifully carved horses with elaborate and elegant saddlery. As well as the traditional and ever-popular dapple greys there are painted rocking-horses in all colours, those with a natural-wood finish, and some covered with real skin. This century has also seen the advent of rocking-horses made of tin, and the use of glass-reinforced plastic and other types of plastic. But this book is concerned with wooden horses, and, by way of an introduction to wooden-horse making, here are three designs for that simplest of wooden toy horse, the hobby-horse.

MAKING HOBBY-HORSES

They are all based on the same pattern for the shape of the head, and will not be beyond the capability of even the novice woodworker with only a few tools at his or her disposal. To start with, you will need a fretsaw or coping saw to cut out the parts, a drill with $\frac{1}{2}$in (13mm) and $\frac{3}{4}$in (19mm) bits, some abrasive paper, and white woodworker's PVA adhesive, and a pair of compasses.

Plate 1.1. (opposite) Traditional fully carved rocking-horse, as described in Chapter 9

Plate 1.2 (inset far left) Slab-sided seventeenth-century-style of rocking-horse, made by the author

Plate 1.3 (inset left) The three sizes of fully carved rocking-horse described in this book

Plate 1.4 (above) The Large carved rocking-horse; this one with a stained and lacquered natural-wood finish

Plate 1.5 (right) Although the mane and tail have gone from this old horse, it is otherwise in remarkably good original condition

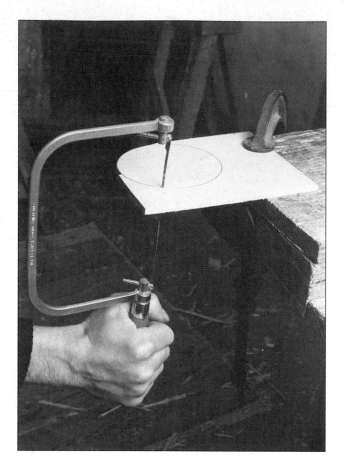

Plate 1.6 Cutting out a plywood hobby-horse wheel with a coping saw

Plate 1.7 Plywood hobby-horse head and connecting piece

The first hobby-horse

In the first design the head, wheel and connecting pieces are all made from ³⁄₈in (9mm)-thick plywood. Birch-faced ply tends to be the best, and a piece 10in x 12in (254mm x 305mm) will be big enough for all the parts. The stick and handle are made from ³⁄₄in (19mm)-diameter ramin dowel, the handle being 7in (178mm) long with both ends sanded to round them over, and the stick 26in (660mm) long (though you can of course vary the length of stick to suit the height of the potential rider). You will also need a short piece of ¹⁄₂in (13mm) ramin dowel approximately 1¹⁄₂in (38mm) long for the axle. It is important that the drill bits mentioned above make holes into which the dowel will fit tightly — dowel does tend to vary a little in diameter between manufacturers.

Make a pattern of the head-shape out of thin card, pencil round it on to the plywood and saw out. Note that you should leave on the piece marked A on Fig 1, at the bottom of the neck. Sand the edges smooth, and mark the position of the eyes on both sides. The eyes can be very simply done by drilling very shallow ¹⁄₂in (13mm) holes, just through the first lamination

of the plywood. Next, saw out a 5in (127mm)-diameter disc for the wheel. Sand the edge to round it over a little, and drill a ¹⁄₂in (13mm) hole through the centre. You will need to enlarge this hole slightly to enable the wheel to spin freely on the axle. Do this by wrapping a piece of abrasive paper round a pencil and rubbing it vigorously through the hole. The connecting pieces are a sandwich of three pieces of plywood glued together. Cut some strips of the plywood to finish 1¹⁄₈in (29mm) wide. For the head-end connecting piece you will need two pieces of this 6³⁄₈in (162mm) long, and one piece 2¹⁄₄in (57mm) long. For the wheel end you will need two pieces 5¹⁄₂in (140mm) long, and one piece 2¹⁄₈in (54mm) long. Mark, saw and sand off a rounded end on each of the four long strips.

Glue the connecting pieces together, making sure that you align the pieces correctly. Cramp them until the glue dries if you have cramps. If not, place them on a flat surface with a very heavy weight on top. Sand smooth all round. The next job is to drill a ³⁄₄in (19mm) hole into the end of each connecting piece for the stick to fit into. This is the tricky bit — the hole

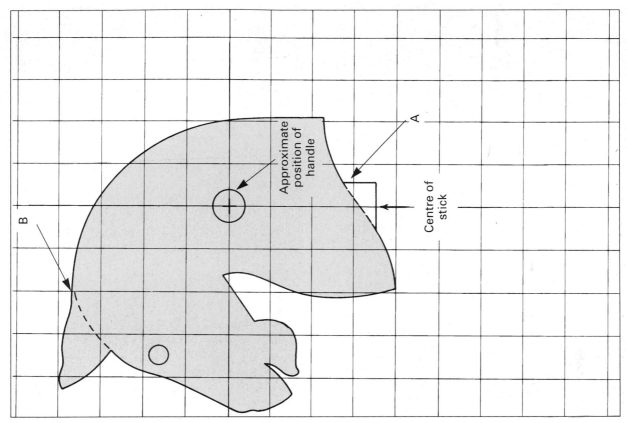

Fig 1 *Scale plan for hobby-horse's head (1in² grid)*

Fig 2 *Scale plan for hobby-horse showing plywood sandwich connecting piece (1in² grid)*

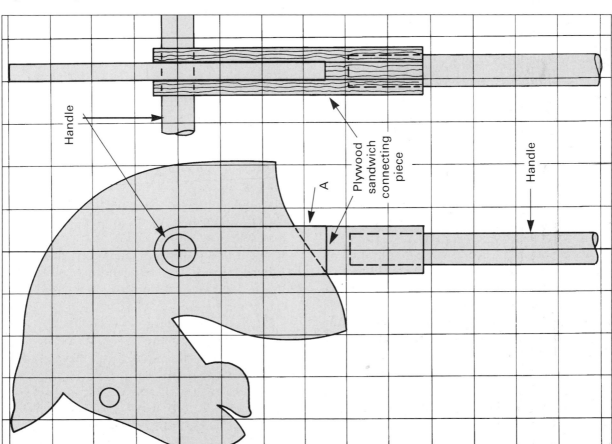

Plate 1.8 Hobby-horse wheels. On the left is a plywood wheel and connecting piece; the other three have solid-wood connecting pieces and wheels

needs to be straight down the middle to a depth of about 1¾in (44mm). A holding vice under a power-drill press is best, but I have done this with a hand drill, judging by eye, with the connecting piece held firmly in a vice, and it is not difficult. But if your drill bit does wander off course and breaks out at one side, you will just have to remake the connecting piece.

Glue the head-end connecting piece on to the neck, so that it is tight up against the piece marked A on the bottom of the neck. Mark and drill the ¾in (19mm) hole for the handle, which passes right through the connecting piece and neck, and glue in the handle. Then glue the stick into its hole in the connecting piece.

Take the wheel-end connecting piece and mark the position for the axle hole. Tuck a piece of scrap ⅜in (9mm) plywood between the two legs of the connecting piece and drill the ½in (13mm) hole for the axle. The gap between the legs of the connecting piece is ⅜in (9mm) — the same as the thickness of the wheel — so obviously if you try to fit the wheel in place like this it will be too tight to spin. What you must do is 'ease the situation' by par-

ing away one lamination of the plywood at the inside of each leg. You will find you can do this quite readily with either a sharp chisel or knife.

Prepare two small wedges as shown in Fig 3, from a piece of scrap wood. Make a saw cut into each end of the axle. Tuck the wheel in position and push through the axle, applying a little glue at each end, but making sure you do not get glue on the wheel. Then apply a little glue to the wedges and tap them into the saw cuts at either end of the axle. Saw off the excess ends of the axle, and glue the lower connecting piece on to the stick, lining up the head and wheel. Sand smooth all round and your hobby-horse is finished, ready for varnishing and/or painting.

The second and third hobby-horses

In the other two versions of the hobby-horse design the head is cut from solid wood 1¼in (32mm) thick, using the same head pattern. No connecting piece is necessary since the stick hole is drilled right into the neck. Solid wood gives you the opportunity to do a bit more shaping on the head. No 2 merely has rounded-over edges and drill-hole eyes, but No 3 is carved or whittled to give a bit more of a three-dimensional horse's head shape and real glass eyes are fitted. Almost any kind of timber will do for these heads, though coarser-grained wood such as red pine is more difficult to carve and has a tendency to split. Tulipwood, basswood or lime are ideal close-grained and relatively easy timbers for carving. When marking out the pattern on the timber, make the direction of the grain run more or less along the direction of the ears — if the grain runs across the ears they will more readily snap off. Also, as well as leaving on the piece marked A in Fig 1 (until after the stick hole has been drilled), it is a good idea to leave a bigger piece of waste wood on the bottom of the neck to give you something to hold on to while carving it.

The shaping or carving can be done with a sharp knife, or carving gouges if you have any. Pencil in a few guide lines before you start to cut into the wood — the shape of the ears, the curve of the cheek and the approximate positions of the eyes and nostrils. The ears are separated with a coping saw, down to the dashed line marked B in Fig 1. Aim to give the head a slight taper from the full width at the eyebrow down to the mouth, with just the nostrils sticking out. The glass eyes are set into shallow recesses with wood filler.

The wheel end needs a connecting piece,

Plate 1.9 The finished hobby-horses, varnished and decorated with coloured tape

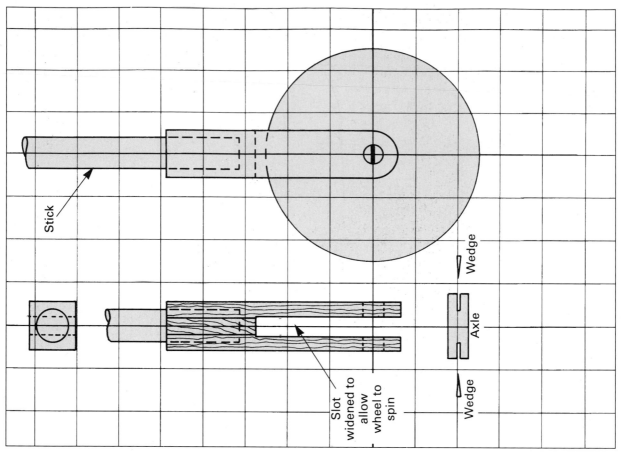

Fig 3 *Scale plan showing plywood sandwich connecting piece for wheel end (1in² grid)*

Fig 4 *Scale plan showing solid wood connecting piece for wheel end (1in² grid)*

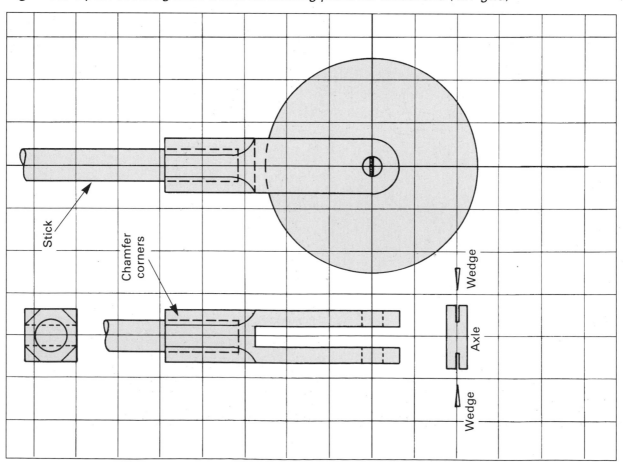

which can be either laminated from plywood as described above, or made of solid wood 1¼in x 1¼in x 5½in (32mm x 32mm x 140mm) cut as shown in Fig 4, and enhanced with some chamfering at the corners. The wheels can also be made of solid wood and, if you have a lathe, can be turned to ensure that they are exactly round and to give them 'tyres'. When you cut the slot for the wheel in the connecting piece, make sure that the wheel has enough clearance to spin. There are lots of variations on the basic hobby-horse; I hope these ideas give you an interesting starting point. When finished, hobby-horses can be either varnished or painted, and may be decorated with ribbons and bows.

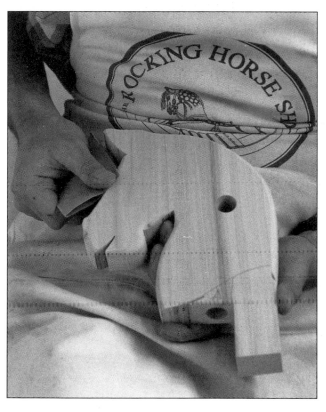

Plate 1.10 Sanding the edges of the 'No 2' hobby-horse head. Note the hole for the stick, and the piece that has been left below the base of the neck to make it easier to hold

Plate 1.11 Carving the 'No 3' hobby-horse head with a penknife

CHAPTER 2
TIMBER AND TOOLS FOR ROCKING-HORSES

CHOOSING TIMBER

It is vital that the timber you use should be good quality and well seasoned. Nothing is more disheartening than to have spent a great deal of time and effort making your rocking-horse only to find that when you bring it into a centrally heated room the joints begin to crack and open up. The best way of ensuring that this does not happen is to have good tight joints and to use properly dried timber. This normally means using kiln-dried timber, since air-dried stock from a timber merchant rarely has a sufficiently low moisture content.

WORKING CONDITIONS

It also helps if you can work on your timber in conditions similar to those in which it will be situated when finished — in other words if your rocking-horse is to be kept in a centrally heated room your workshop should be heated likewise. I know this is a bit of a tall order and may not be practicable. Do recognise, though, that if you make your rocking-horse in a damp shed outside, and then bring it into a well-heated room, you are quite likely to have problems with cracking. Timber, especially kiln-dried timber, will take up moisture from the atmosphere, so if you have to store it for some time try to keep it in a dry place. I know one maker who kept and worked on his horse in a corner of the living room while the rest of the family watched TV in the same room, disregarding the dust and woodchips. You may not have such an understanding spouse as that maker, but you have to get your priorities right!

TYPES OF TIMBER

Where plywood is specified (for the Toddler's horse in Chapter 3), you are unlikely to have any problems with moisture content, but it is advisable to work and store plywood in dry conditions or it may de-laminate and warp, particularly the cheaper grades. For carved wooden rocking-horses you will need a timber which is relatively easy to carve, stable when

assembled, and available in the various thicknesses and widths specified in the cutting list. Many of the old-time rocking-horse makers used yellow pine, which carves well, for the head and body, with legs in beech, for its greater strength. Alternatively we recommend jelutong or basswood for head and body. Both are excellent close-grained carving timbers, especially for the beginner, being relatively soft and easy to cut into. Again, you should use something tougher, like beech or maple, for the legs.

For a traditional painted dapple-grey finish it does not matter if you mix the timbers. But if you intend going for a natural-wood finish then you will probably want to use the same type of timber throughout. Mahogany carves well and is tough enough to be used for the whole horse, including legs. Tulipwood (American poplar), sycamore and lime all carve well and are normally plantation-grown or from renewable resources, so avoiding the use of tropical hardwoods. Tulipwood in particular is an excellent carving timber, readily available at present; it has a good-looking grain pattern which takes stain well, or it can be painted. Many other hardwoods may be both suitable and available — you should take your timber merchant's advice on this. Rocking-horses have been made entirely from beech or oak, but these are very much harder to carve, and I cannot see a great deal of virtue in making life much harder for yourself than it need be.

On the whole you should avoid using red pine or deal, such as is supplied for the building industry, since this tends to be of coarser grain and poorer quality, though first-quality Scandinavian or Russian red woods may be used with satisfactory results. Some makers have successfully used second-hand timber, and I have seen a beautiful horse made from old pitch pine obtained from a demolition contractor, but you do have to watch that rusty old nails do not ruin the cutting edges of your tools.

When designing the plans in this book I tried to use dimensions that followed standard timber

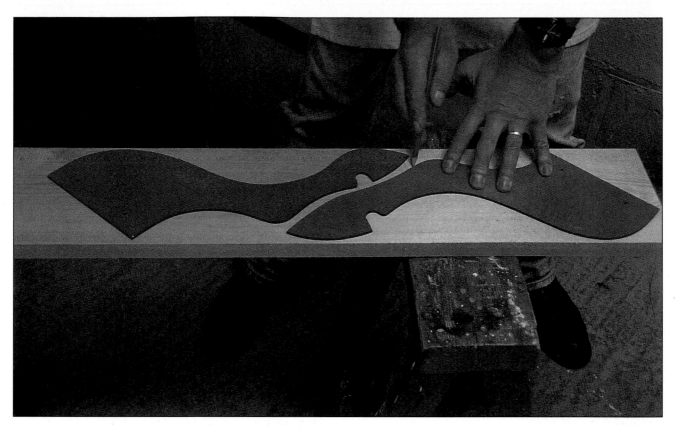

Plate 2.1 Full-size patterns (in this case for the Swinger-horse legs) are used to mark the shapes on to the timber. Note how the patterns overlap to economise on timber

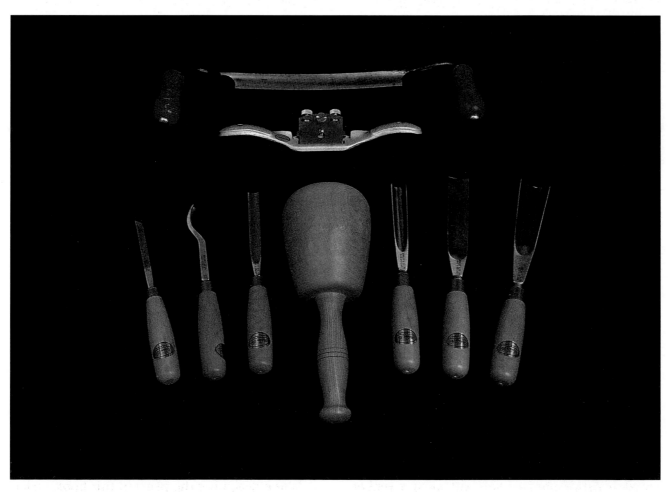

Plate 2.2 Rocking-horse carving tools: a drawknife (top) and spokeshave, six gouges and a carver's mallet

sizes, but it has not always been possible. In the cutting lists, therefore, where non-standard sizes are specified, or where the specified widths or thicknesses prove to be unavailable from your timber merchant, you may have either to cut down a piece to suit, or to laminate together two or more pieces to achieve the required dimensions.

The cutting lists give the finished dimensions (ie after planing) of all the timber required. A reasonable allowance for fitting the patterns of the odd-shaped pieces (eg legs) on to the timber has been made. Again, according to the availability of timber, you may vary the widths and lengths specified — for example, if you obtain timber wider than that specified for the legs, then the length required will be less since you will be able to overlap the leg patterns more on the board.

PREPARING PATTERNS

You will need to make patterns or templates for all the shaped parts: head and neck, ear and eye pieces, neck-muscle blocks, legs and leg-muscle blocks. First, make actual-size paper patterns of these shapes by scaling up from the drawings in this book (or use the actual-size drawings available — see Appendix 2) and transfer them on to thin hardboard or card, using tracing or carbon paper, and cut them out. Position the patterns carefully on the timber so that the direction of grain conforms as near as practicable to that shown on the drawings, pencil round them, and then cut them out, keeping your sawcut just outside the pencil line and taking care to leave in place any cramping noggins or bevelling allowances.

It is possible to use a hand-held jigsaw (sabersaw) to cut out all the shaped parts, particularly for the smaller horses where no part is thicker than $1\frac{3}{4}$in (45mm). I know of one maker, who evidently loves a challenge and is not afraid of hard work, who cut out all the parts by hand with a coping saw. But the simplest and most accurate way is to use a bandsaw. A small benchtop bandsaw capable of cutting up to 3in (75mm)-thick timber is quite adequate. We normally use a $\frac{3}{8}$in (9mm)-wide blade in the bandsaw, which will go round most of the curves, but you will need to drill holes where the bends are tight, and through the mouth.

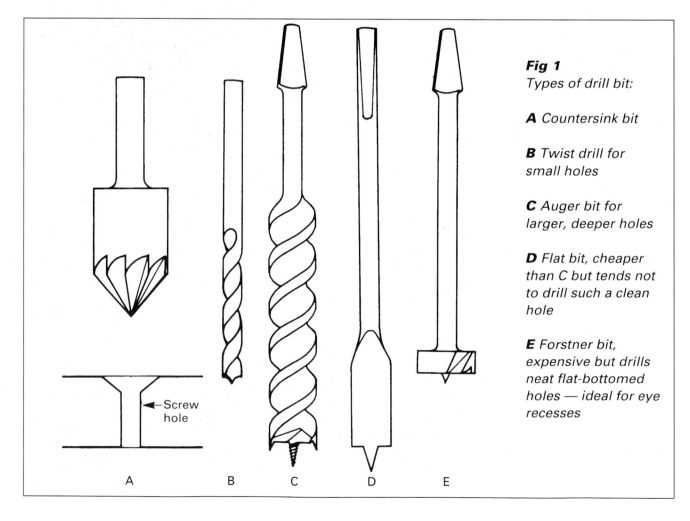

Fig 1
Types of drill bit:

A *Countersink bit*

B *Twist drill for small holes*

C *Auger bit for larger, deeper holes*

D *Flat bit, cheaper than C but tends not to drill such a clean hole*

E *Forstner bit, expensive but drills neat flat-bottomed holes — ideal for eye recesses*

←Screw hole

A   B   C   D   E

TOOLS: HAND AND POWER

When you come to assembling the various parts at least six F-type sliding cramps (or small sash cramps) are required. For the small horse you can manage with only four of these cramps, but it is advisable to have more since they do help to make the assembly easier and speedier; as one of the basic rules of woodwork says: 'You can never have enough cramps'. We recommend sliding F-type cramps since they are efficient, easy to use, and relatively inexpensive. Four 4in (100mm) G-cramps are also needed for carved horses. Cramps are not used at all for the Toddler's rocking-horse or the Swinger rocking-horse (Chapters 3 and 4).

The ordinary woodworking tools that are essential include: a try square, a pair of compasses, a smoothing or jack plane, coping and panel saws, a screwdriver, and a drill with a selection of bits. Also abrasive paper in various grades — 80, 120 and 180 grit, and 240 and 360 grit if you require a super-smooth natural-wood finish.

Now to consider gouges for carving; it is best to use a large one with a deep sweep for roughing out and another largish one with shallower sweep for getting rid of the deeper ripples, and then a few smaller ones for carving the details. We recommend the following six gouges: No 8 – 1¼in (32mm) alongee gouge; No 4 – 1in (25mm), No 9 – ⅝in (16mm) and No 5 – ½in (13mm) straight London Pattern gouges; No 2 – ⁵⁄₁₆in (8mm) straight corner chisel; No 30 – ⅜in (10mm) spoon gouge. You may well be able to manage with fewer or different ones, but these six will equip you to carve any rocking-horse. Some woodcarvers, and by no means only novices, have difficulty keeping their gouges good and sharp as they work. For an explanation of an easy method of grinding and honing carving gouges, see Appendix 1.

You will also need a mallet to use with the bigger gouges. A round woodcarver's mallet is best, since it will wear evenly all round as you use it. It should have a comfortable ash handle, a beech or maple head, and not be too heavy — around 22oz is quite heavy enough. A few other hand-tools will aid the carving: a round and a curved Surform or rasps will help you to shape some of the more awkward curves around the neck and to remove gouge marks; a drawknife (though it takes a bit of getting used to) is useful for slicing off the waste wood around the

Plate 2.3 Using a spokeshave to smooth off the neck of a large horse

body and neck; and a spokeshave helps you to smooth the slow curves. A router, with rounding-over and chamfering cutters will be useful, for the rounding of edges in the Swinger and Little Red Rocker designs, and for cutting the chamfers on stands. But if you do not have one these can readily be done by hand with rasp, plane or spokeshave.

There are a number of power carving tools on the market which enable you to produce wonderful carvings in no time at all, if you believe the advertisements. These include pneumatic or electrically driven gouges, rotary rasps with flexible drives, power files, and carving or rasping attachments for angle grinders. I have tried several of these and there is no doubt that they can be extremely useful. Some of the angle-grinder attachments in particular are very effective at removing a lot of waste wood very quickly. However, they tend to be rather fierce and require absolute concentration. You need face and arm protection from flying wood chips, since one small slip could spell disaster (even if only to your carving), and they are no fun at all to use. So, on balance, and in the interests of 'real' woodcarving, I would recommend the traditional mallet-and-gouge approach. It may be a little slower but it is a lot more satisfying and why, after all, be in such a hurry?

However, one part of rocking-horse making where power assistance can be welcomed is sanding down. Most of the head and under the chin will have to be sanded by hand, in order to get into all the awkward places, but for the rest of the horse foam-backed drum-sanding attachments for your electric drill, and pad or orbital finishing sanders, can greatly ease what is otherwise a long and laborious process.

CARVING IN 3D

It is the carving, particularly the carving of the head, which makes most prospective rocking-horse makers apprehensive. The head involves the most detailed carving, and it is here that the expression and character of the horse is defined. If you can make a satisfactory go of the head then carving the rest of the horse will be quite straightforward by comparison. And like most practical endeavours the carving of the head is much more difficult in the anticipation than in the accomplishment (really!). Most people achieve good results, even those who have done little or no carving before, and frequently amaze themselves. 'I didn't think I could do it,' they say with pride, 'but just look at this!'

Before starting on the carving study the photographs in this book to familiarise yourself with the procedure and the shapes to aim at. Some people find it helps them to understand and feel the contours involved if they make a practice model in clay or play dough. It may also help to look closely at real horses, but do not let this confuse you. What we are making here is a traditional-style rocking-horse, and not a carving of a real horse. The rocking-horse tends to be stylised, often with simplified forms, and although it must be instantly and unambiguously recognisable as a horse, it need not have all the features and contours of a real horse. What may be absolutely right for a rocking-horse can often be quite unlike the real thing. And conversely, carvers who try to make a realistic horse may find that it is visually unsatisfactory if mounted as a rocking-horse. A knowledgeable horselady once asked me, 'Why is it that your rocking horses do not look like real horses?'. I replied simply that it is because they are not real. There is a tradition in rocking-horse making which I follow (though not too slavishly); it works and it looks right and I recommend it.

All of the drawings, photographs and instructions given in this book are aimed at ensuring that you achieve a satisfactory result; that is a rocking-horse that will be both fascinating for you to make and a delight for its riders. I can give you the information that I have found, by experience, to be helpful in achieving this. But I cannot, nor would I want to, take the tools from your hands. In the end the rocking-horse will be yours, and it will be different from anyone else's. Even starting from the same basic plan it is quite remarkable how different and variable can be the results. Let this be a source of pleasure for you in your own achievement, rather than a reason for frustration that you are not getting it 'correct'. If you do get frustrated with it and feel that it is just not coming right for you, leave it alone for a while before taking up your tools for another go. It will certainly come good in the end.

ADHESIVES AND FILLERS

A few words about adhesives: for many years we have used Cascamite glue, with no problems. This is a strong, waterproof urea-formaldehide adhesive — a white powder mixed with water — and we use it throughout the construction. Joints do need to be cramped since the glue takes at least six hours to set hard (faster in hot weather), and we usually leave glued joints overnight before removing the cramps. It is a good idea to scrape off any surplus glue before it sets; otherwise it could blunt your gouges or even chip them — it is rock hard when completely set. Other types of glue, such as PVA woodworkers' adhesive, have also been used with satisfactory results, particularly for the Toddler's horse.

Some carvers get rather sniffy about the use of woodfillers, but you will need a filler with which to set in the glass eyes, and probably also to fill any blemishes or cracks. The best type to use is a two-part, paste-plus-catalyst filler of the sort intended for use on wood. Mix in a polythene container or on a scrap of wood using a palette knife or an old dinner knife. Thoroughly mix a small amount of catalyst with the paste according to the instructions (the proportions are usually 1:30), and then apply it as quickly as you can, since it begins to harden within ten minutes or so (quicker in warm weather). Avoid using motor-car-body-type fillers, which are too hard and inflexible, or decorators' plaster fillers, which are too brittle or too grainy.

HOLDING DEVICES

A carved rocking-horse is an awkward shape to hold securely while you are working on it. The best holding device is a proper carver's chops mounted on a carving bench, such as you can see in Plate 2.4. The carver's chops is simply a wooden vice with rather high and relatively narrow jaws, usually faced with leather or cork, with a steel screw that allows the jaws to open up to about 12in (305mm). The carver's bench is relatively tall and thin; the carving is thus at a convenient working height and you can work all round it without having to constantly change its position. The bench has a platform base, upon which you stand, so your own weight helps to keep the bench immovable. If you are intending to do a fair bit of woodcarving it is time well spent to make yourself a carver's chops and bench such as this. Plans are available — see Appendix 2.

However, if you do not wish to go to the trouble of making a chops and bench for what may be only a one-off carving project, you can make do with an ordinary woodwork bench and vice, provided the jaws will open far enough to hold the body. Some makers use a DIY-type workbench or 'Workmate', or a large saw-horse on to which the work is clamped; or the horse can be laid on sandbags while you carve it.

Plate 2.4 Carver's chops: a wooden vice ideal for holding work secure as you carve

CHAPTER 3

A TODDLER'S ROCKING-HORSE

Based on the seventeenth-century slab-sided style of rocking-horse, this design is ideal for younger riders. Although at first glance it may not be your idea of a 'proper' rocking-horse — not having legs or a mane and tail and so on, it does have a lot to commend it. Because it is low to the ground children are able to climb on unaided from a very early age, about ten months or so, and this is a great boon to parents. With larger rocking-horses children are usually two years or older before they are big enough to be able to climb on or off without assistance, and even then probably need an adult standing by to help. As soon as they are on they want to be off, and vice versa. So it is a relief to have a rocking-horse that little ones can enjoy unaided.

The rider has complete control, and may wish to just rock very gently. But if he or she is bolder and wants to really make it rock, it will reward him or her with a very exciting ride. I have seen several mothers jump with anxiety as their youngsters rocked this horse to the extremity of its rockers. But they have little need for concern since it is virtually impossible to overturn.

TOOLS

The other thing that commends this design is that it really is quite straightforward to make. It requires only a jigsaw or small bandsaw to cut out the parts, a smoothing plane, a hand drill with countersink and 5/32in (3.5mm) bits for the

screw holes and 3/4in (19mm) bit for the handle hole, a screwdriver, a sharp bradawl, white woodworkers' PVA adhesive, and abrasive paper. You will also need 30 x 1in (25mm) counter-sunk-head wood screws. The head and neck form a simple 'silhouette' shape and are described first, but an alternative carved-head version is also given, as an opportunity for novice woodcarvers.

PLANS AND TIMBER

First, prepare full-size patterns or templates out of card, for all the shaped parts, and prepare your timber according to the cutting list below. The head, rump, foot-rests and seat battens can

Cutting list

	Thickness x width x length			Thickness x width x length		
	Inches			**Millimetres**		
Head and neck	1¼ x 8	x	12	32 x 203	x	305
Rump	1¼ x 3¾	x	6	32 x 95	x	152
Foot-rests	¾ x 2¾	x	14	19 x 70	x	356
Seat battens (x 2)	¾ x 1¾	x	15⅜	19 x 45	x	391
Seat	⅜ x 6⅞	x	18⅞	9 x 175	x	480
2 Rocker panels						
and seat back	⅜ x 24	x	36	9 x 610	x	914
Cross-pieces (x 2)	¾ x 9½	x	9½	19 x 241	x	241
Handle	¾ diam x	7		19 diam	x	178

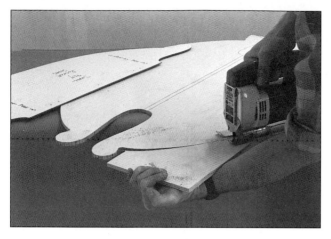

*Plate 3.1 Cutting out rocker panels with a jigsaw —
the hardboard pattern can be seen behind*

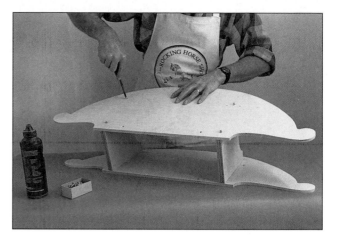

*Plate 3.2 Glueing and screwing rocker panels
to cross-pieces*

be pine, sycamore, lime, tulipwood, or any other suitable timber that your timber merchant can supply. The seat, rocker panels and seat back are cut from ³⁄₈in (9mm)-thick plywood — birch-faced ply is usually the best. The cross-pieces can be cut from ³⁄₄in (18mm)-thick plywood or blockboard. The handle is a length of ramin dowel, with the ends rounded over with abrasive paper. Place the patterns carefully on the wood and pencil round them. Note that the seat back is marked on to the same piece as the rocker panels, and the straight top edges of the rocker panels are to be bevelled, so leave a small allowance for this. If you mark the positions of all the screwholes on the patterns you can prick-mark them through on to the wood with the bradawl.

CONSTRUCTION

Saw out all the shapes and drill the screwholes, and the ³⁄₄in (19mm) hole through the neck for the handle. You will notice that on the rocker panels the rockers project further from the seat at the front than at the back. This is to help to balance the toy better when in use. Hold the two rocker panels together and mark one 'left' and the other 'right'. Countersink the screwholes on the outside of each panel so that the screwheads will sit flush or just below the surface of the ply — except for the three holes for the foot-rest which are countersunk from the inside surface.

Glue and screw on the seat battens so that they project about ¹⁄₈in (3mm) above the rocker panel and plane off the bevel to an angle of 10°. Do not worry about getting this angle exact at this stage — it can be adjusted later, after the rockers are assembled. Now glue and screw on the cross-pieces, making sure that the tops of the cross-pieces are flush with the tops of the rocker panels and that the screws enter the cross-pieces centrally. Adjust the bevelling along the top so that the seat will sit flat down.

Take the seat and countersink from the top

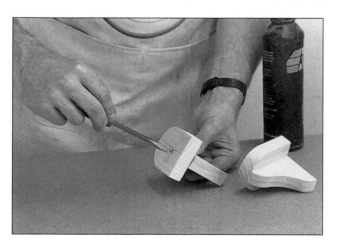

Plate 3.3 Assembling foot-rests

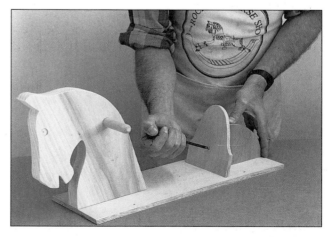

*Plate 3.4 The silhouette head and the rump have been
glued and screwed to the seat from underneath and the
seat back is being fixed in position*

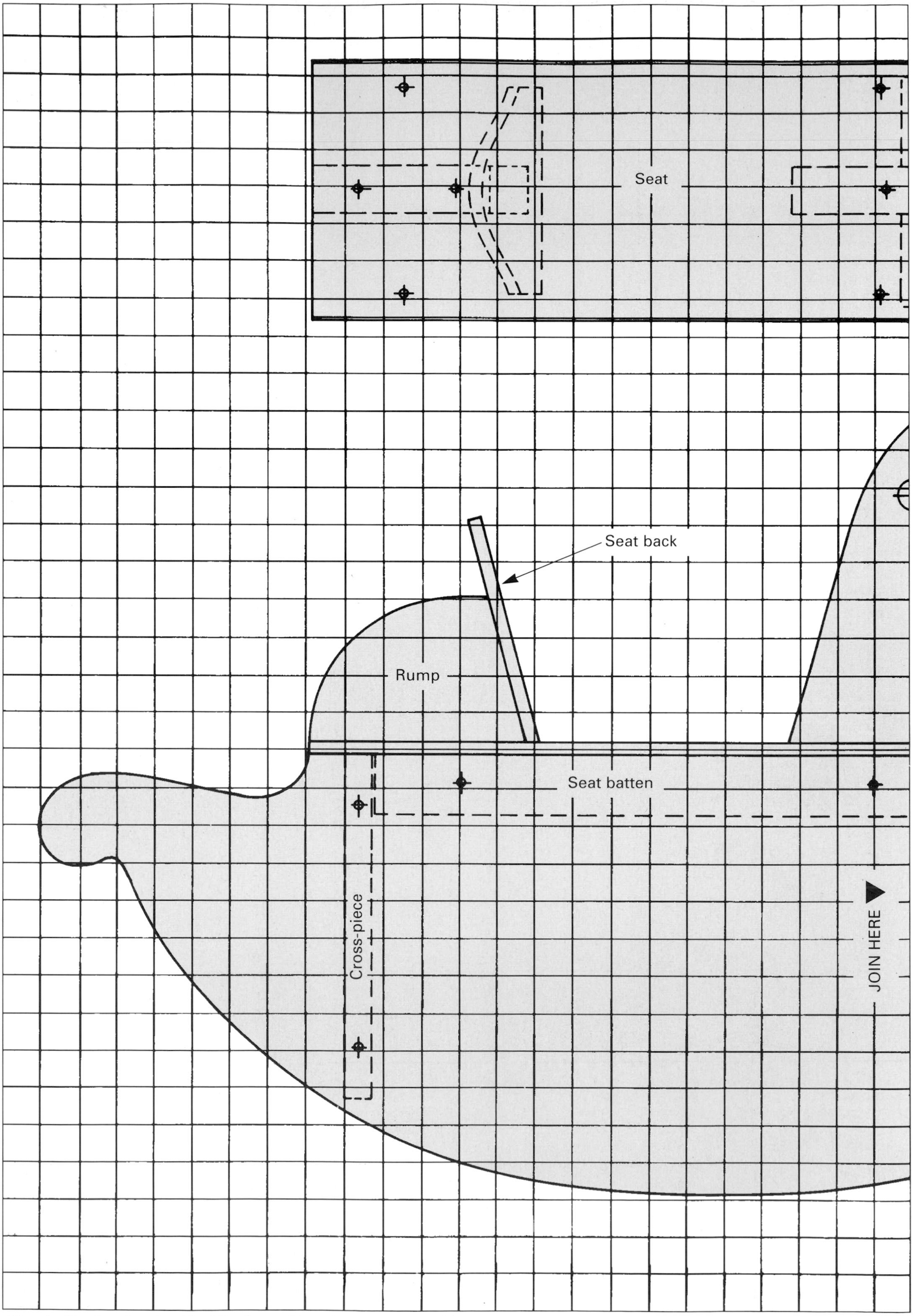
Seat
Seat back
Rump
Seat batten
Cross-piece
JOIN HERE

Fig 1 *Scale plan for Toddler's rocking-horse (1in² grid)*

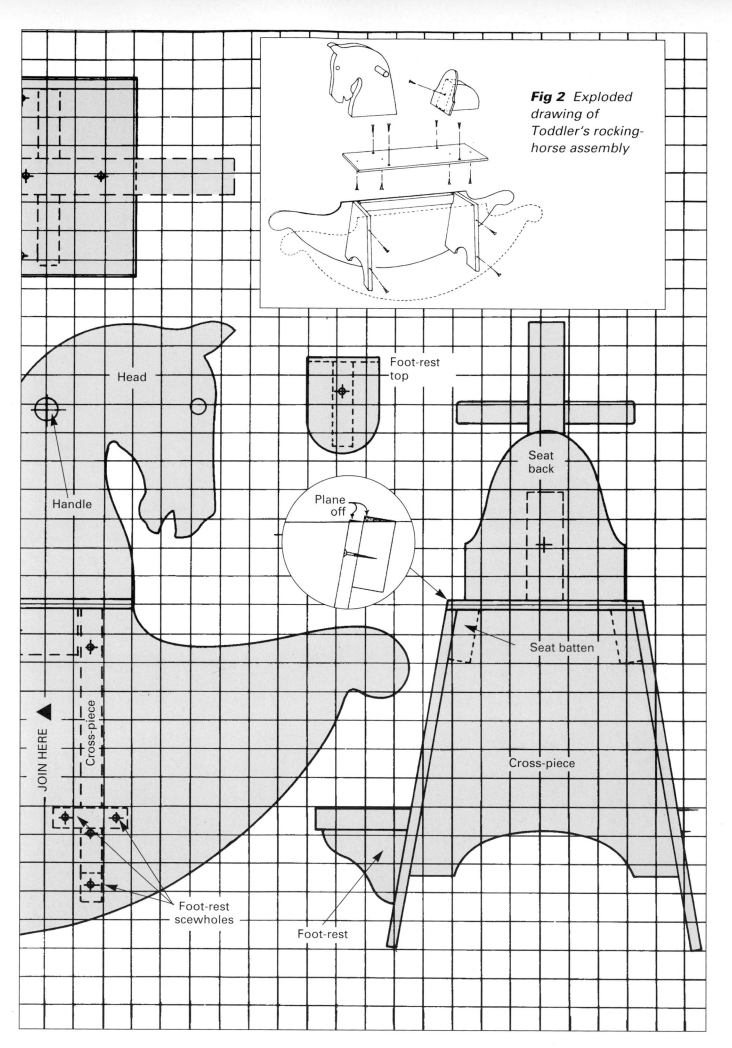

Head

Handle

JOIN HERE ◄

Cross-piece

Foot-rest
scewholes

Fig 2 *Exploded drawing of Toddler's rocking-horse assembly*

Foot-rest
top

Plane
off

Seat
back

Seat batten

Cross-piece

Foot-rest

for the four screws that will secure it to the seat battens, and from underneath countersink the two holes to fix the neck, and the two to fix the rump. Screw the seat temporarily in position (without glue) so you can plane off the edges either side until they are flush with the rocker sides.

Unscrew the seat and to it glue and screw the rump, centrally, at the back. The bottom of the seat back is bevelled (the angle is 15°) with the plane to fit neatly down on to the seat when it rests back against the rump. Drill and countersink the single screwhole in the seat back, and glue and screw in position.

On the head, the eyes can be simply indicated by drilling a shallow hole, or they can be painted on later. Glue and screw on the head and neck centrally at the front, and glue the dowel handle centrally in its hole. Glue and screw the seat assembly down on to the rocker assembly, making sure that you get the head at the front. Sand off thoroughly all round.

The end of the top of each foot-rest is bevelled at 10° with the smoothing plane. The two parts of each foot-rest are glued and screwed together. Make sure that the inner face of the foot-rests will lie flat to the rocker sides, by rubbing them on a flat sheet of abrasive and glue and screw in position, from the inside. After a final sand-down all round to remove any roughness and sharp corners your rocking-horse is ready to be varnished and/or painted.

AN ALTERNATIVE CARVED HEAD

Fitting a carved head to this rocking horse not only enhances the appearance, it is also an interesting woodcarving project — particularly for those who have previously done little or no carving. The shape of the head and neck is the same as for the silhouette version above, but thicker timber is used and extra pieces are glued on to the sides. Sycamore, lime or tulipwood, basswood or jelutong are all excellent carving woods. Prepare the timber as follows:
Make card patterns of the shapes and mark them on to the timber. Drill the hole for the

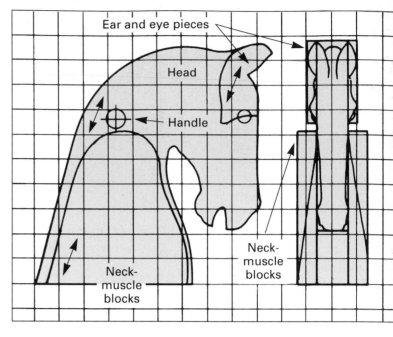

Fig 3 *Scale plan of alternative carved head (1in² grid)*

handle and glue on the neck-muscle blocks and ear and eye pieces either side as shown. You will need at least three 4in (100mm) G-cramps for this. The bottom of the neck must be planed and sanded flat so that it can later be fitted down neatly on to the seat.

For the carving you will need at least two carving gouges: a No 4 – 1in (25mm) and a No 9 – ⅝in (16mm) straight London pattern, though a few more will certainly be useful; see Chapter 2 for more information on carving tools and approaches to carving. Start by clamping the head upside down in your vice so that the bottom of the neck is uppermost. On this pencil-mark the shape of the base of the neck, which is an egg shape, 'thick end' towards the front. With the largest gouge and mallet chop down at the waste side of this line. Watch that the wood does not split away too much (take a little at a time) and guide the cutting edge of the gouge so that the front and rear of the neck begin to take on a rounded shape and the muscle blocks at the sides taper in towards the neck. Screw a small block of scrap wood on to

Cutting list: *Carved Head for Toddler's Rocking-horse*

	Thickness x width x length			Thickness x width x length		
	Inches			**Millimetres**		
Head and Neck	1¾	x 8	x 12	45	x 203	x 305
Neck-muscle Blocks	¾	x 5¾	x 15	19	x 146	x 381
Ear and Eye Pieces	⅜	x 2¾	x 8	9	x 70	x 203

Plate 3.5 Glueing on the ear and eye pieces and neck-muscle blocks for the carved head

Plate 3.7 Separating the ears with a coping saw. Note the pencilled guide lines

Plate 3.6 Carving the taper of the neck. Note the block screwed on to the base of the neck which will be used to hold the work in the vice

the base of the neck. This gives you something to hold on to (in the vice) when you turn the head the right way up.

Pencil-mark a centre line all round the head (to help guide you in keeping the symmetry), the shapes of the ears looking from the front (a coping saw will be useful to cut away the waste wood between the ears), the curve of the cheek, and the approximate positions of the nostrils. With the 1in (25mm) shallow gouge cut back the corners at an angle for the nostrils and pencil in the shape of the nostrils and pare the wood back all round.

As you carve, study the accompanying photographs, which should give you a good idea of the shapes and contours to aim at. Work steadily, cutting a little from each side in turn and remember that a horse's head has no corners.

Plate 3.8 Cutting along the line of the cheek with a straight chisel. Note how the carving of the nostrils and eye pieces has progressed

Plate 3.9 The rough carved head

Plate 3.10 Now it has been sanded smooth, the nostrils and ears hollowed out, and the glass eyes and handle have been fitted. It is ready to fix on to the seat

The ears are pointed, but should not be left sharp. Unless you have chosen a particularly hard timber you should hardly need a mallet; instead push the gouge across the timber in a paring, slicing action that cuts small pieces away cleanly. It is important to keep your gouges sharp (see Appendix 1). And if you feel your gouge is digging in too deep, stop and try again from another angle. Once you have rough-carved the head to a shape with which you can be pleased, sand down thoroughly all round.

Glass eyes really set off the head well. They are $\frac{5}{8}$in (16mm) in diameter and are set into shallow recesses about $\frac{1}{8}$in (3mm) deep with woodfiller. Make sure both eyes are at the same height and cut the recesses slightly larger than the eye. Put some soft woodfiller (the same colour as your wood) into the recess and push in the glass eye so that the filler squeezes out all round. Smooth off the excess filler, and the eye is then gripped firmly and neatly in position. Glue the handle in its hole, and glue and screw the head on to the seat, centrally, at the front.

In order to keep the design simple I have not used any accessories other than eyes, but of course it would be quite possible to fit a padded seat or decorative bridle. The finished horse can be either clear varnished or painted. The rocker panels can be enhanced with some fancy painting, or by affixing pictorial transfers. It is a sturdy and attractive little rocking-horse, and will give great pleasure to its young riders.

Plate 3.11 At nine months, Lynn can almost reach the foot-rests. This white-painted version also has painted eyes

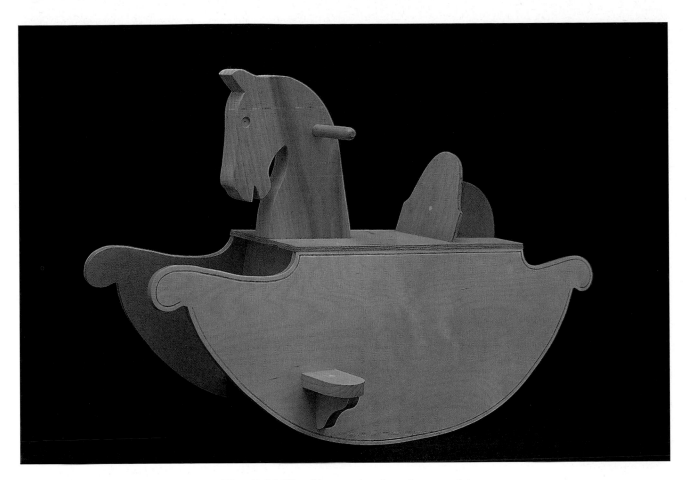

Plate 3.12 The silhouette-head version complete

Plate 3.13 The carved-head version complete

CHAPTER 4
THE SWINGER
ROCKING-HORSE

The idea behind this design is a simple-to-make, good-looking rocking-horse for children up to the age of six or so. Mounted on a swing-iron safety stand so that it has a proper rocking action, it is easy to make because the construction involves no carving at all. After the parts have been cut out, the only shaping that the design calls for is the rounding over of some of the edges. This rounding over is most easily accomplished, if you have one, with a ½in (13mm)-radius cutter in a router, or it can be done quite simply after assembly with the aid of a rasp and abrasive paper. You will also need a smoothing plane, a drill with ¾in (19mm), ³⁄₁₆in (5mm), ⅛in (3mm) and countersink bits, and a pair of compasses.

PLANS AND CONSTRUCTION METHOD

First, prepare the timber. The horse can be made entirely of pine or tulipwood except for the handle, which is ramin dowel, and the body sides, which are birch-faced plywood. The cutting list below gives the actual finished sizes required in order: thickness, width, length and number of pieces. Due allowance has been made for fitting the patterns of the odd-shaped pieces — ie head and neck and legs etc — on to the timber, but for the seat, leg-fixing blocks and body sides the length given is the actual finished length required.

Note that the two pieces for the head and neck need to be glued together edge to edge to make a piece approximately 11½in x 12in (292mm x 305mm). Cramp the two pieces together with sash or sliding F-cramps, or you can make up a simple cramping jig by nailing two pieces of scrap wood on to your bench and wedging the pieces to be glued tightly between, as shown in Fig 2. Place some newspaper under the glued join to prevent it from becoming stuck to the bench; this can be cleaned off after the glue has set.

Make actual-size patterns out of thin card or hardboard for the head, rump, back-rest, legs

Cutting list

	Thickness x width x length				Thickness x width x length			
	Inches				**Millimetres**			
Head and neck (x 2)	1³⁄₈	x 5³⁄₄	x	12	35	x 146	x	305
Handle (round dowel)	¾ diam	x 7			19 diam	x 180		
Back-rest	⁷⁄₈	x 4½	x	4¼	22	x 114	x	108
Rump	1¾	x 1¾	x	5	45	x 45	x	127
Seat	1¾	x 5³⁄₄	x	21	45	x 146	x	533
All four legs	⁷⁄₈	x 6	x	72	22	x 152	x	1,830
Leg-fixing blocks (x 2)	1³⁄₈	x 4½	x	5	35	x 114	x	127
Body sides (plywood) (x 2)	¼	x 4	x	11	6	x 100	x	279
Foot-rest	¾	x 1¾	x	17	19	x 45	x	432

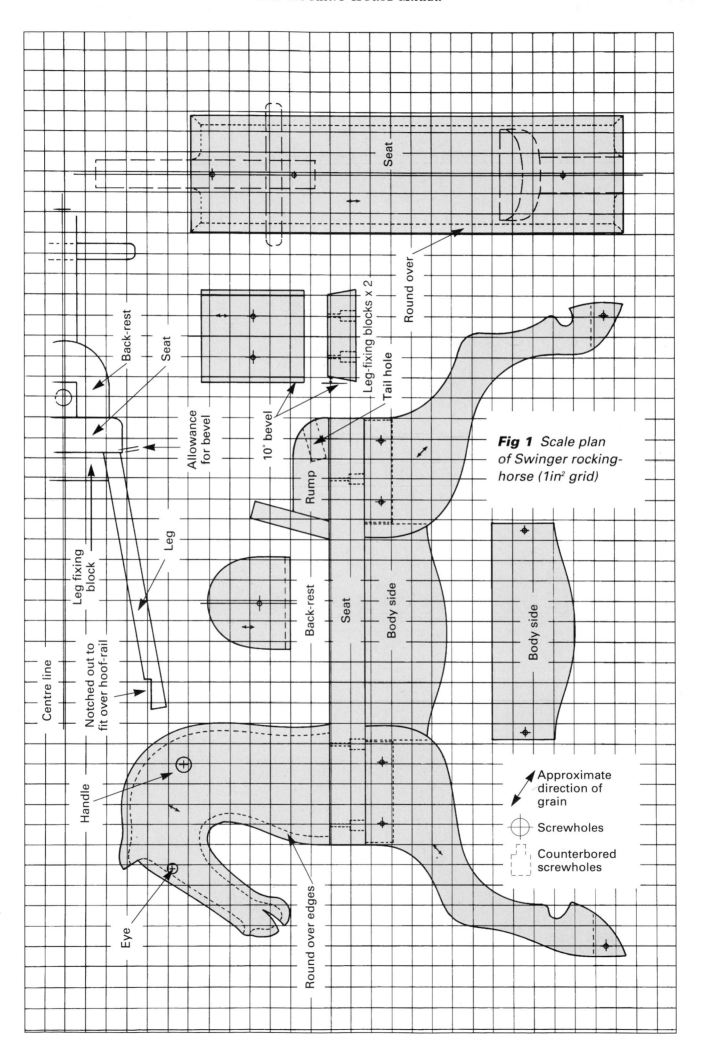

Fig 1 Scale plan of Swinger rocking-horse (1in² grid)

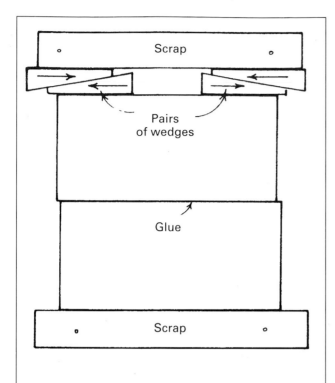

Fig 2 *Jig for glueing-up pieces for head (not to scale)*

and body sides, and transfer the shapes on to the timber. Note that the tops of the legs are to be bevelled at 10°, so an allowance of at least ³/₁₆in (5mm) should be left on the straight top edges as indicated on the drawing. When you have cut out all the parts, mark on them the positions of the screwholes. The screwholes on the seat and leg-fixing blocks are counterbored as shown in the drawing. Drill a ³/₄in (19mm) hole through the neck for the handle, and into the rump for the tail.

The sides of the leg-fixing blocks are bevelled to 10°, as are the straight tops of the legs, and the bottom of the seat back is bevelled to 15°. Mark the bevel on the wood and carefully plane off with the smoothing plane or, if you have a bandsaw with a tilting table, you can bandsaw the bevels and then clean up the bandsaw cuts with the plane.

As mentioned above, if you have a router with a rounding-over cutter, you can do the rounding over of the top edges of the seat and round the head before assembly. Note the places where the edges are not rounded over:

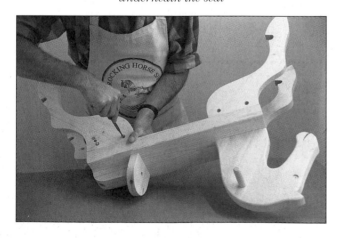

Plate 4.1 Screwing on the seat back. The rump and the neck have been glued and screwed in position from underneath the seat

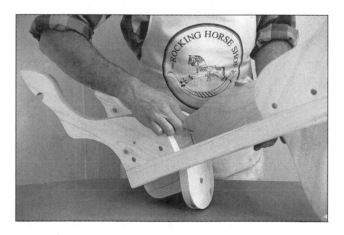

Plate 4.2 Screwing the leg-fixing blocks to the underside of the seat

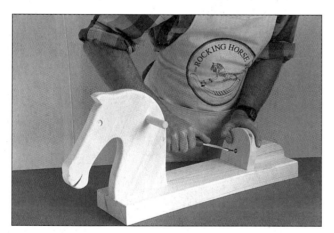

Plate 4.3 Screwing on the legs

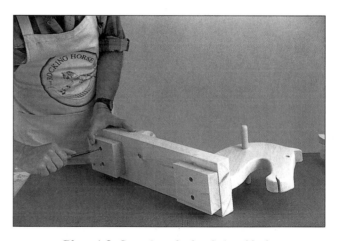

Plate 4.4 Fixing body sides to the insides of the legs

Plate 4.5 *The finished Swinger rocking-horse. The tail has been fixed into its hole and the horse mounted up on its stand*

the front of the ears, the nostrils, and on the seat where the head and rump are to be fixed down. Glass eyes are set into shallow recesses about $5/8$in (16mm) diameter and $1/8$in (3mm) deep. Cut the wires from the glass eyes (if they have them) and push them into the recesses with soft pine-coloured woodfiller so that the filler squeezes out all round, then clean off the excess filler leaving the eyes firmly set.

For the assembly, use white PVA glue and countersunk steel woodscrews: 2 x $2^{1}/2$in (64mm) 10g for fixing neck to seat, 14 x $1^{3}/4$in (45mm) 10g (1 each for fixing rump to seat and back-rest to rump, 4 for screwing leg-fixing blocks to seat and 8 for securing legs to leg-fixing blocks). You should counterbore for the screws through the seat and leg-fixing blocks. The rest can be countersunk so that their heads sit just below the surface to be filled with wood-filler, or you may like to set them a little deeper and cover the screwheads with wooden plugs. Of course, you will need a suitable drill bit and plug cutter, $1/2$in (13mm) diameter, to do this. You will also need 4 x $1/2$in (13mm) 4g screws, 2 to fix on each of the body sides.

When fixing on the head, rump and leg-fixing blocks make sure that they are aligned centrally on the seat and that the bevels on the leg-fixing blocks will allow the legs to fit in neatly under the seat. Also, an obvious point, but easily overlooked in the excitement of getting it all together, make sure that the front legs are at the front. Round the ends of the handle with abrasive paper and glue into its hole in the neck. When the glue has set and you have filled or plugged all the visible screwholes, give the whole thing a thorough sand-down, taking care not to scratch the glass eyes.

The hooves need to be notched so that they fit neatly over the hoof rails on the stand. For details of how to do this, and of how to make the stand, refer to Chapter 7. When the hooves have been notched you can drill a screwhole through each hoof and screw on temporary hoof rails with $1^{1}/4$in (32mm) 8g screws. The temporary hoof rails enable you to varnish the hooves and prevent them getting chipped. The horse can now be varnished (or painted if you prefer). Give it two or three coats of clear polyurethane varnish, lightly sanding down between coats.

Plate 4.6 Swinger horse almost complete. The screwholes are yet to be filled or plugged and the glass eyes fitted

I usually varnish right over the glass eyes and then scrape the varnish off them when it has dried. This is easier than brushing carefully round the eyes, and the varnish does not stick very well to the glass anyway. The bridle and reins are made up using $3/8$in (9mm)-wide red-leather strap, a piece about 56in (1,425mm) long will be enough for both, and they are fixed to the head with $1/2$in (13mm) 4g roundhead brass screws. The tail, which is usually of synthetic hair, is glued into its hole and secured by tapping in a small wooden wedge underneath. That completes the horse which can now be mounted up on its stand. This horse does not have stirrup irons; instead a foot-rest is screwed on to the hoof rails so that it projects evenly at either side. It is positioned so that when the horse is rocked right forward the foot-rest does not quite reach the stand post. Altogether, this is a super little rocking-horse which will give a great deal of pleasure to children.

Plate 4.7 The glass eyes have been fitted, and after varnishing the simple bridle and reins are screwed on to the head

CHAPTER 5

THE LITTLE RED ROCKER

This design combines the simple construction of the Swinger with a carved head, neck and upper body. It is an excellent rocking-horse for children up to the age of six or so, and the carved elements are nicely complemented by the red-leather bridle and saddle. Choose a timber which carves readily — the horse in the accompanying photographs is made out of tulipwood — and prepare your timber according to the cutting list below.

PLANS AND CONSTRUCTION METHOD

Make full-size patterns of all the parts and mark them out carefully on the timber, then bandsaw out. Note that the two ears and two eye pieces shown on the plan are cut from offcuts of the piece from which the head and neck and the two neck-muscle blocks are cut. The grain should run in the direction of the arrows on Fig 1. The ears are bandsawn to 1in (25mm) thickness and the eye pieces to $\frac{3}{8}$in (9mm) thickness. Also leave an allowance of $\frac{3}{16}$in (5mm) on the top straight edges of the legs for the 10° bevel.

The plan shows counterbored screwholes in the seat for fixing it to the head and rump; however, you may prefer to use fluted-dowel pegs, with centring markers to locate the holes (see Appendix 1 for details of how to use these), in which case the cramping noggin on the neck

Plate 5.1 The eye pieces have been glued on. Now the ears are glued and cramped in position

Cutting list

	Thickness x width x length			Thickness x width x length		
	Inches			**Millimetres**		
Head and neck						
Neck-muscle blocks (both)	$1\frac{3}{4}$	x $8\frac{3}{4}$	x 23	45	x 222	x 603
(Ears and eye pieces)						
Seat	$1\frac{3}{4}$	x $5\frac{3}{4}$	x 21	45	x 146	x 533
Rump	$1\frac{3}{4}$	x $5\frac{3}{4}$	x 8	45	x 146	x 203
Leg-fixing blocks (x 2)	$1\frac{3}{8}$	x $4\frac{1}{2}$	x 5	35	x 114	x 127
Legs (all 4)	$\frac{7}{8}$	x 6	x 72	22	x 152	x 1,830
Body sides (x 2)	$\frac{1}{2}$	x $4\frac{1}{2}$	x $10\frac{7}{8}$	12	x 114	x 276
Battens (x 2)	$\frac{3}{4}$	x $\frac{3}{4}$	x $10\frac{7}{8}$	19	x 19	x 276

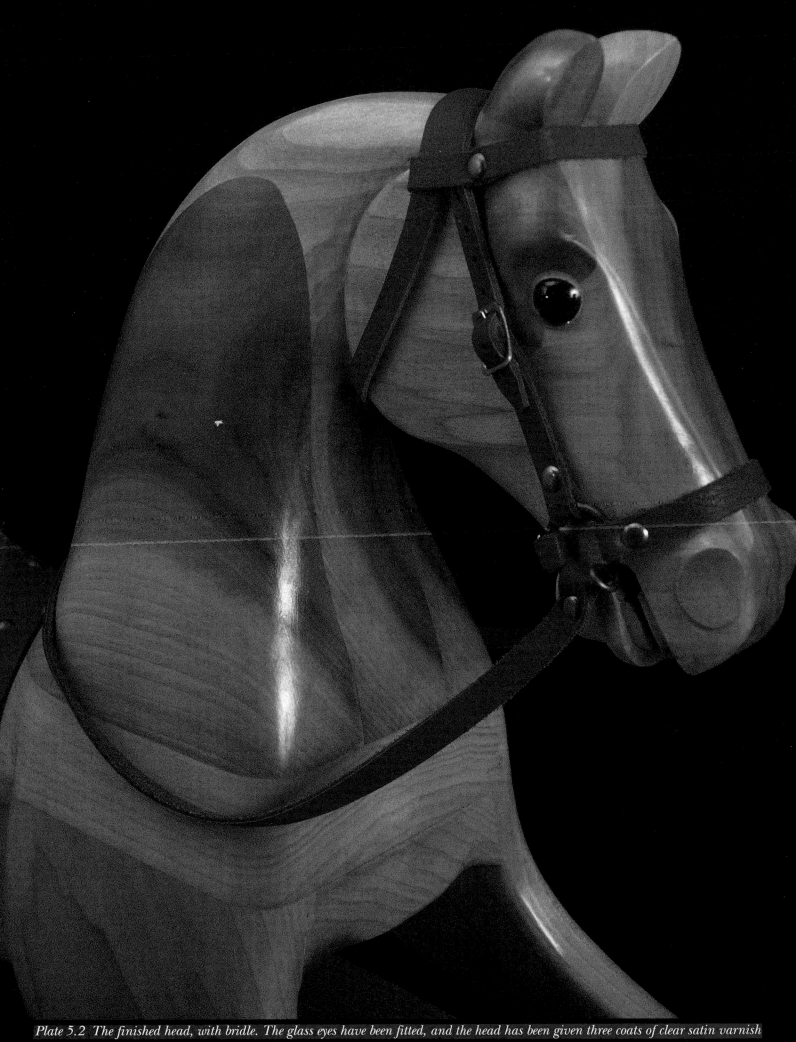

Plate 5.2 *The finished head, with bridle. The glass eyes have been fitted, and the head has been given three coats of clear satin varnish*

Plate 5.3 Both neck-muscle blocks and the rump can be glued on in one go if you have enough cramps

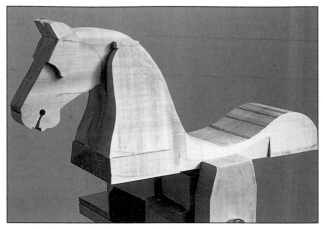

Plate 5.4 The waste from the neck-muscle blocks, and the curve of the seat and rump, have been bandsawn. If your bandsaw will not handle this depth of cut you will have to cut away the waste with a large gouge and mallet

will aid the cramping down. Cramping noggins are also left on the tops of the neck-muscle blocks, and the ears.

First glue and cramp the eye pieces to the head, making sure that the top edges are flush with the top of the head. When set, remove the cramps and sand the top flat with coarse (80 grit) abrasive wrapped round a flat block of wood, and similarly sand the bottoms of the ears flat, so that they will fit down neatly on to the top of the head. The outside edges of the ears are flush with the outside edges of the eye pieces. Since sticking-out ears are always vulnerable to knocks, you may like to strengthen the joint with a ³⁄₁₆in (5mm) fluted-dowel peg 1in (25mm) long. Glue on the ears.

When you fix down the head and neck ensure that it is positioned centrally on the seat. You may need to plane the bottoms of the neck-

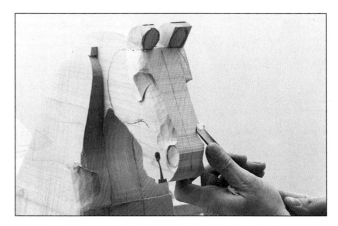

Plate 5.5 Start to carve the head with a large shallow gouge

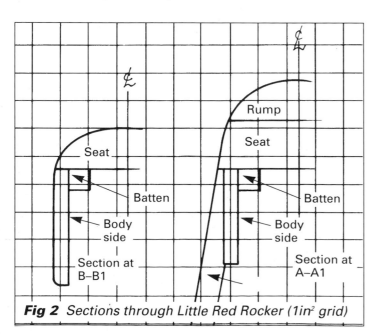

Fig 2 *Sections through Little Red Rocker (1in² grid)*

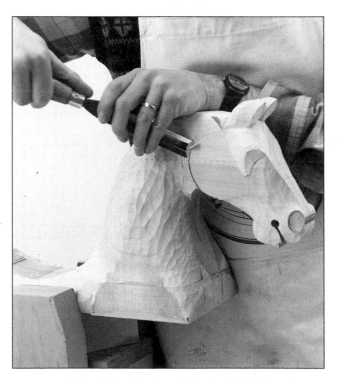

Plate 5.6 Carving in to the cheek line

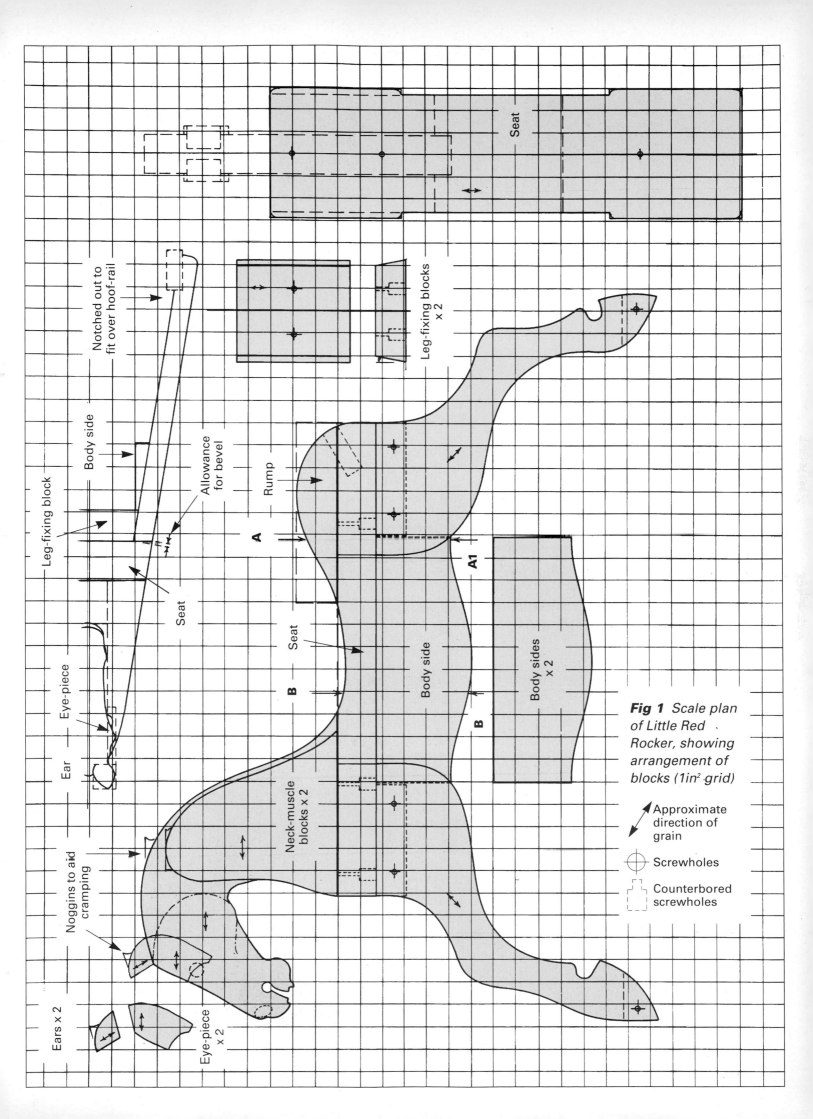

Seat

Notched out to fit over hoof-rail

Body side

Leg-fixing block

Allowance for bevel

Seat

Rump

A

A1

Leg-fixing blocks x 2

Neck-muscle blocks x 2

Body side

Body sides x 2

B

B

Seat

Eye-piece

Ear

Noggins to aid cramping

Ears x 2

Eye-piece x 2

Fig 1 *Scale plan of Little Red Rocker, showing arrangement of blocks (1in² grid)*

Approximate direction of grain

Screwholes

Counterbored screwholes

Plate 5.7 Rounding over the rump. See how the carving of the head and neck has progressed, and note that the carving stops short of the bottom edges of the seat

Plate 5.8 The tops of the legs are notched out so that the body side is fitted at right angles to the underside of the seat and flush with the outside edges of the seat

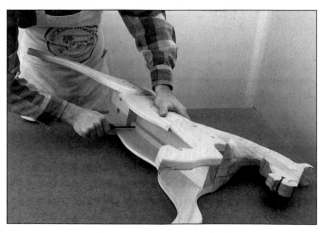

Plate 5.9 Screwing on the body sides

muscle blocks to make them fit neatly on to the seat and neck at either side, then glue and cramp them in position. The fronts of the neck and neck-muscle blocks should all be flush with the front edge of the seat. Glue on the rump, which is not shaped at all prior to assembly.

Pencil in the curved shape of the seat and rump. If you have a bandsaw that will cut to a depth of 6in you can turn the horse on its side and bandsaw off the waste from rump and seat. And if your bandsaw table will tilt, set it to 10° and bandsaw down each side, keeping the seat full width 5¾in (146mm) at the bottom. This angled saw cut is rather deep through the neck and your bandsaw may not be big enough to cope, in which case you can carve away the waste with your biggest gouge and a mallet.

Before you proceed with the carving, pencil in some guidelines: a centreline to help you keep the symmetry, the shapes of the ears, the approximate positions of eyes and nostrils, and the curve of the cheek (which starts at the base of the ears and curves back round to the throat). The waste around the ears can be removed with a coping saw.

Take the 1in (25mm) shallow gouge and pare back the wood at an angle where the nostrils will be, and pencil in the oval shape of the nostrils. Cut back all around the nostrils until they stand proud. Then carve off the corners above the eye, up towards the base of the ears. The eye piece remains at its full thickness just above the eye (the eyebrow), but below the eye it is carved to run smoothly into the surrounding wood. With a straight chisel cut along the line of the cheek then pare back the wood on the waste (neck) side of this line. Cut deeper towards the throat — the front of the neck in the area of the throat will eventually be rounded. Below the cheek the head is gradually tapered down to the mouth, which finishes about 1⅜in (35mm) wide.

Carefully cut away the mouth to reveal the teeth, and round over the corners at the back of the lower jaw. Work steadily taking a little from each side in turn and stand back from time to time to examine your progress. The neck-muscle blocks should be carved to run smoothly into the neck which is rounded over at the top. You can use a bigger gouge and mallet here, and also to round over the rump and seat. At this stage do not carve right down to the lower corners of the seat block. When you are getting close to the final roughed-out shape, leave the carving while you fix on the legs and body sides.

Plate 5.10 The complete Little Red Rocker. The glass eyes have been fitted and it has been given three coats of clear satin varnish before fitting the saddle, tail and buckling on the bridle and mounting on its stand. Ready to rock!

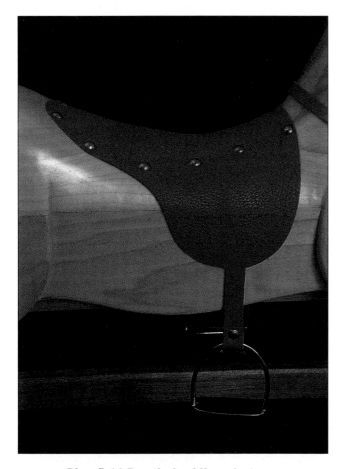

Plate 5.11 Detail of saddle and stirrups

Plate 5.12 Rear view showing the tail fitted into its hole

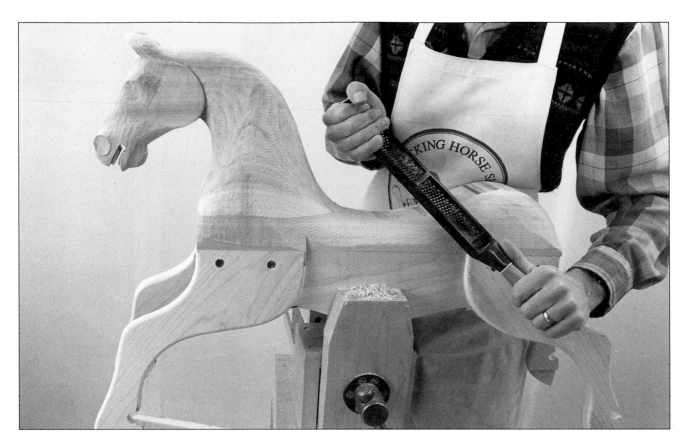

Plate 5.13 A piece of scrap wood has been wedged between the body sides to prevent them from being crushed in by the vice. Here a half-round Surform is being used to complete the rounding over of the body, prior to sanding smooth

Check that the outer face of the legs will be flush with the lower edge of the seat and glue and screw on the leg-fixing blocks centrally to the underside of the seat. The ends of the leg-fixing blocks should be flush with the ends of the seat. Then screw on the legs temporarily (without glue) while you mark for the notches which are sawn from the inside of each leg. These notches enable the body sides to be fitted at right angles to the underside of the seat and flush with the edge of the seat in the middle (where the seat is narrower).

The edges of the legs and the lower edges of the body sides are rounded over. This can be most easily accomplished before assembly with a rounding-over cutter in a router, if you have one. Take care not to round over that part of the leg which will be against the leg-fixing block. If you do not have a router, do the rounding over with a rasp and abrasive paper after assembly. Glue and screw the legs and body sides in position. To prevent the body sides from being crushed in when you put the horse in your vice, tuck pieces of scrap wood tightly between them. Now you can finish the carving.

A half-round Surform is very useful for removing gouge marks and further rounding the rump, seat and neck which should run smoothly down to the legs and body sides. The rounding of the corners of the legs is carried on up the corners of the seat to run smoothly into the curve of the neck and rump. When you have achieved a satisfactory shape, sand smooth all over, starting with a fairly coarse abrasive like 80 grit, then progressively finer papers — 120, 180, and 240 grit until you lose all blemishes, tool and scratch marks. Fill or plug the screw-holes and drill a ³⁄₄in (19mm) hole for the tail. The hooves will need to be notched to fit over the hoof rails on the stand. For details of how to do this and of how to make the stand, turn to Chapter 7.

Fit a pair of ⁵⁄₈in (16mm)-diameter glass eyes by cutting recesses slightly bigger than the eyes, and about ³⁄₁₆in (5mm) deep, and set the eyes in with woodfiller which is smoothed off all round. The horse can then be varnished — three or four coats of a satin-finish varnish will look good, sanding down lightly between coats.

A pair of small stirrup irons are riveted on to a length of ³⁄₄in (19mm)-wide leather strap 21in (533mm) long. This is laid over the horse's back towards the front of the saddle and nailed on in the middle. The simple saddle is cut from a piece of red leather and has ¹⁄₂in (13mm)-thick foam-rubber padding underneath, as shown in

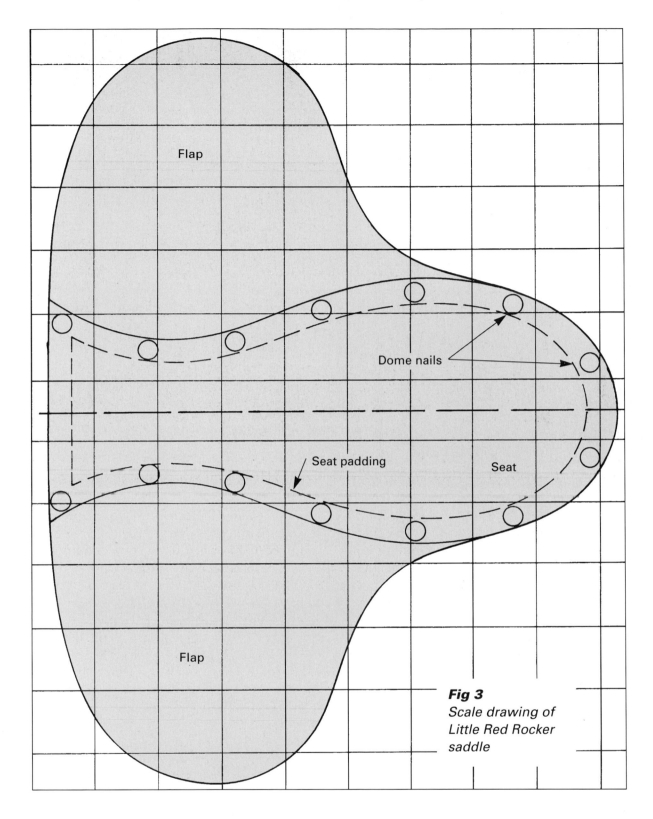

Fig 3
*Scale drawing of
Little Red Rocker
saddle*

Fig 3. Before fitting the saddle, damp the leather a little with water to make it more amenable to being pressed over the contours of the horse, and nail in place with ½in (13mm) brass domehead nails spaced evenly along the crease lines and round the back.

The tail, which is usually of synthetic hair, is glued into its hole and secured with a small wooden wedge tapped in underneath so it is out of sight. The bridle and reins are made up from red-leather strapping. The bridle has little brass buckles and a brass bit, so is simply buckled on to the head. For details of bridle-making refer to Chapter 11. The Little Red Rocker is now ready to be lifted on to the stand (see Chapter 7 for further details of this) where it is secured to the hoof rails with either 1¼in (32mm) no 8 screws or ³⁄₁₆in (5mm) bolts and nuts. It is finished, a delightful and impressive little horse. All it needs now is a rider.

CHAPTER 6
A SMALL TRADITIONAL CARVED ROCKING-HORSE
for mounting on a safety stand

The Victorian style of fully carved rocking-horse was traditionally made in many sizes. In our experience children will normally be 2 to 2½ years old before they are big enough to climb unaided on to a carved rocking-horse of any size; smaller children may well need assistance both to mount and to keep their balance. This design has a body 18in (457mm) long, about the smallest size which can actually be ridden, and will suit children up to 5 years old or so. After this age they are getting rather big for it and tend to ride their dolls on it rather than themselves.

Apart from being a rideable toy, this rocking-horse is a delightful and decorative artefact which will enhance almost any room — and it is a fascinating woodworking project. The design has been kept as simple and straightforward as possible and the construction involves no complicated joints. If you read Chapter 2 before starting, and study the following method carefully, you should have no difficulty in achieving a pleasing and satisfactory result.

The order of procedure for making the horse is as follows: selecting and preparing timber; preparing patterns of all shaped parts; drawing patterns on to the timber and cutting out parts; glueing ear and eye pieces to head; carving the head; rough carving the legs; glueing-up the rest of the horse; carving the body and neck; sanding down.

ASSEMBLY

Tracing off and cutting out
Position the patterns carefully on the timber and pencil round them. Try to ensure that the direction of grain conforms to that shown in Fig 1. Note that certain patterns (eg the legs) will need to be positioned with some parallel overlap in order to minimise wastage.

Cutting list

	Thickness x width x length			Thickness x width x length		
	Inches			**Millimetres**		
Head and neck	1¾	x 8¾	x 16	45	x 222	x 406
Neck-muscle blocks (both)	1¾	x 5¾	x 19	45	x 146	x 483
Eye and ear pieces (both)	⅜	x 2¾	x 9	10	x 70	x 230
Lower- and upper-body blocks (x 2)	1¾	x 5¾	x 18	45	x 146	x 457
Middle-body blocks (sides) (x 2)	1¾	x 3¼	x 18	45	x 83	x 457
Middle-body blocks (ends) (x 2)	1¾	x 3¼	x 2¾	45	x 83	x 70
Legs (all four)	⅞	x 5¾	x 48	22	x 146	x 1,220
Leg-muscle blocks (all)	⅜	x 4¾	x 24	10	x 121	x 610
Saddle block	¾	x 1¾	x 5	19	x 45	x 127

Plate 6.1 The finished Small horse

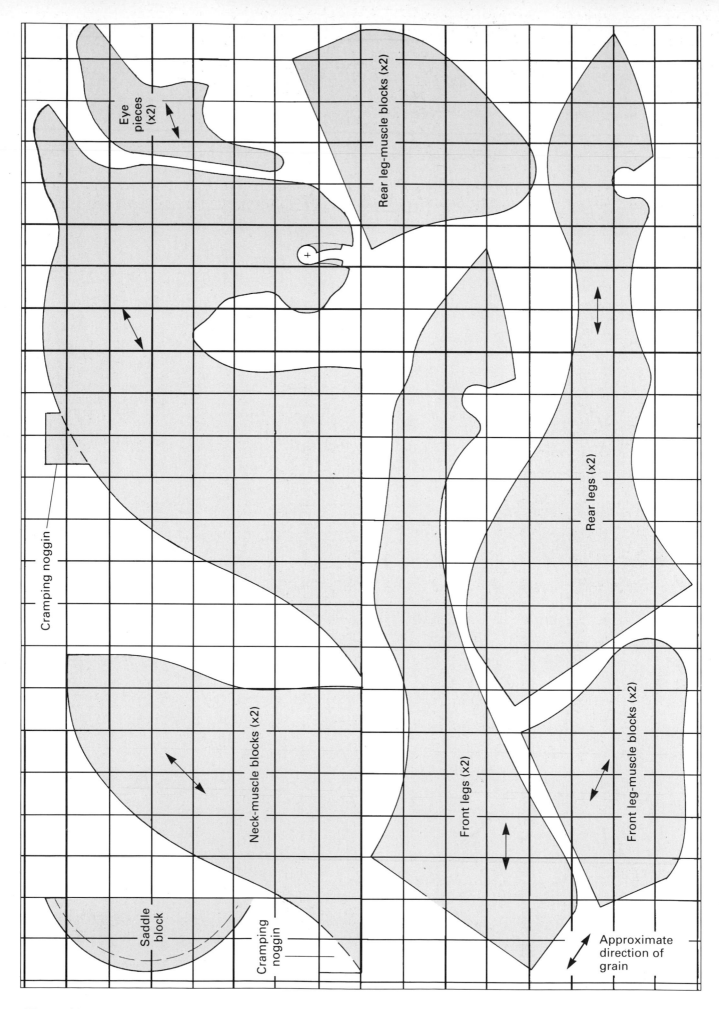

Fig 1 *All shaped parts for Small carved horse on swing-iron stand (1in² grid)*

Eye pieces (x2)

Rear leg-muscle blocks (x2)

Cramping noggin

Rear legs (x2)

Neck-muscle blocks (x2)

Front legs (x2)

Front leg-muscle blocks (x2)

Saddle block

Cramping noggin

Approximate direction of grain

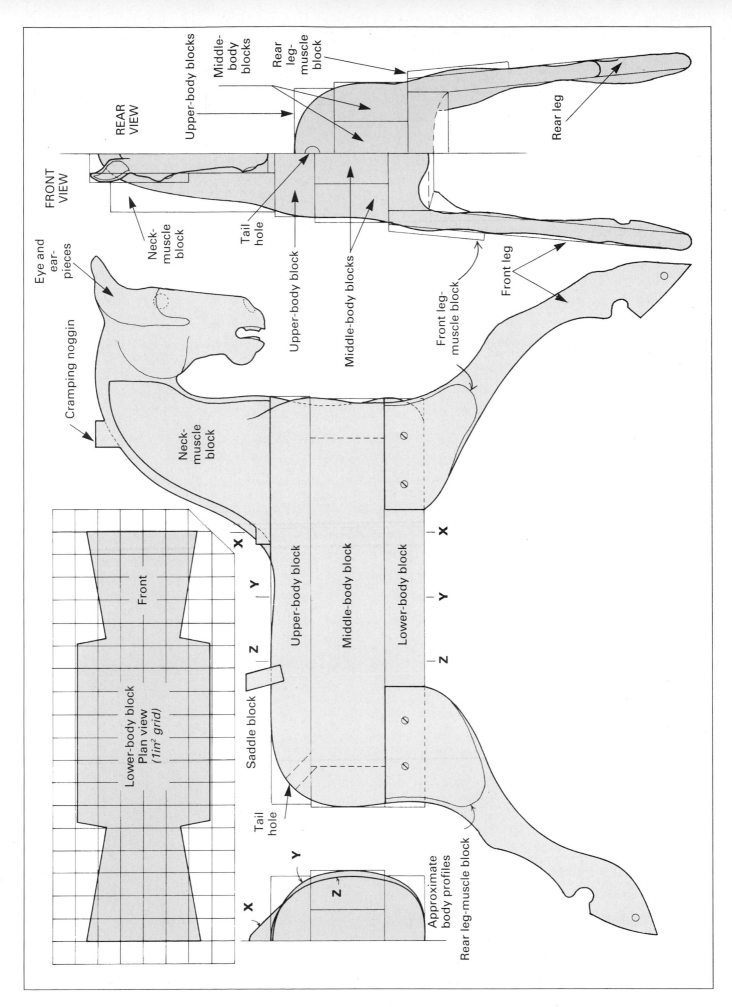

Fig 2 *General arrangement of blocks for Small rocking-horse*

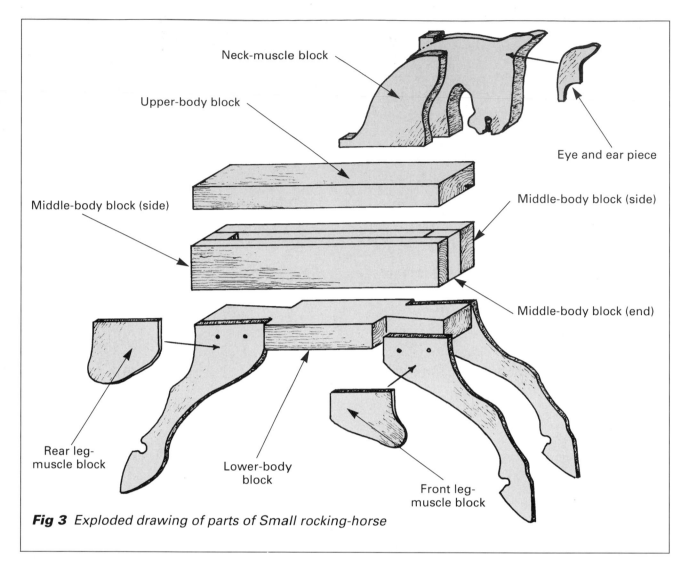

Neck-muscle block

Upper-body block

Eye and ear piece

Middle-body block (side)

Middle-body block (side)

Middle-body block (end)

Rear leg-muscle block

Lower-body block

Front leg-muscle block

Fig 3 *Exploded drawing of parts of Small rocking-horse*

Bandsaw out the shapes, keeping the sawcut just outside the pencil line. We normally keep a ³⁄₈in (10mm)-wide blade in our bandsaw and this will saw round almost all the curves. But where the curve is very tight, such as under the chin, you will need to drill one or two ¹⁄₂in (13mm) holes to allow the blade to turn. Also, drill a ¹⁄₂in (13mm) hole for the mouth in the position shown on the plan, and ³⁄₄in (19mm) holes to form the very tight curves just above each hoof. Make sure that you leave the cramping noggins in place on the neck and neck-muscle blocks — these are to aid the assembly later. The upper- and middle-body blocks are not bandsawn or shaped at all prior to assembly.

Glueing the eyes and ears

Glue the eye and ear pieces to the head, one at each side. The head is carved before it is fixed to the rest of the horse — it is easier to handle like this. So once the glue has set on the eye and ear pieces, prepare to carve your head!

Plate 6.2 Ear and eye pieces glued and cramped both sides of the head

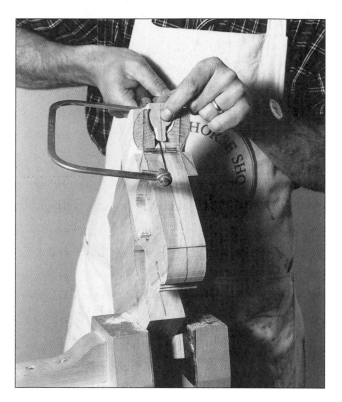

Plate 6.3 Separating the ears with a coping saw

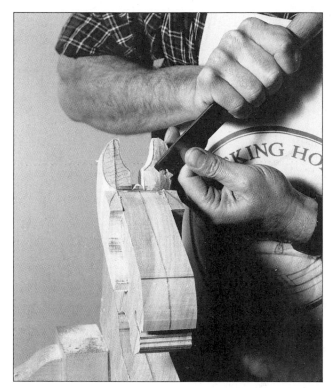

Plate 6.4 Starting to shape the ears with a large shallow gouge

Carving the head

Pencil in some guidelines: a centreline (to help you keep the head symmetrical), the outline of the ears looking from the front, the approximate positions of the eyes and nostrils, and, on each side, the curve of the cheek. Carry the top line of the cheek on either side on to the front and across to join in the middle; this line marks the bottom of the ears. With the coping saw cut along this line at each side, through the ear and eye piece, almost to the glue line. Also with the coping saw cut away the waste around the ears. It is wise to cut well on the waste side: you can always trim more off later if necessary but it is less easy to stick it back on again — this comment, of course, applies to all carving.

When carving, you must cut with the grain of the wood. You can also cut across the grain, but not against it, because the cutting edge will want to follow the grain and will dig in too deep. If this happens (and sometimes it is difficult to tell at a glance which is the best way to cut), you should withdraw the gouge and try from another angle. If you do not do this, and try to force the gouge against the grain, the cutting edge will continue to dig deeper and the wood may split. Work slowly and steadily, carving a little from each side in turn to keep the symmetry. Unless your timber is very hard, you will probably be able to carve the head without using the mallet. Hold the gouge handle firmly in one

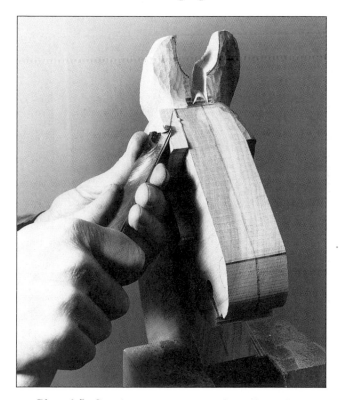

Plate 6.5 Carving away corners above the eyebrow

hand and guide the cutting edge with the other, pushing it across the wood with your thumb in a slicing action that removes small clean slivers at each cut.

Secure the head so it is looking up at the ceiling, take up the 1in (25mm) shallow gouge and

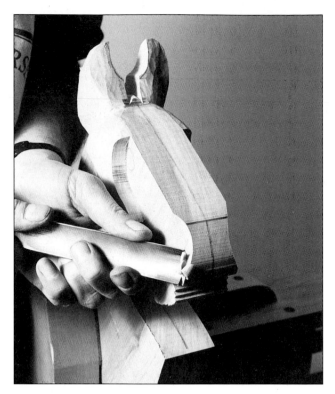

Plate 6.6 The nostrils are carved so that they angle back at each side

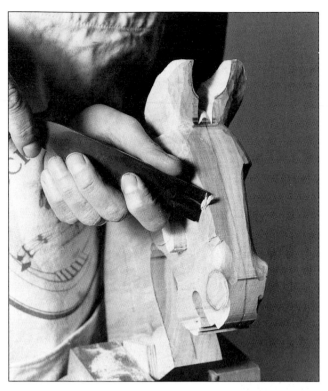

Plate 6.7 The head tapers from eyebrow to mouth, with just the nostrils remaining proud

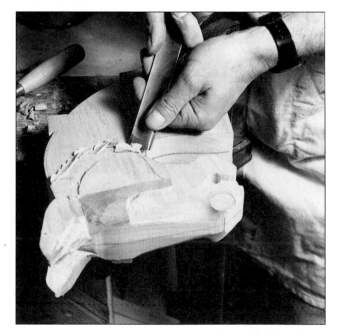

Plate 6.8 Cutting back along the curve of the cheek. Note how the cheek line runs into the base of the ears

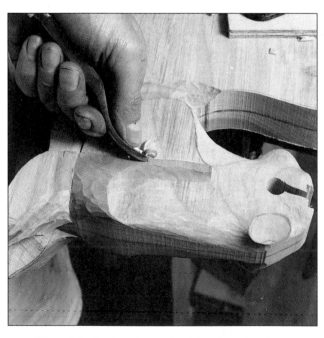

Plate 6.9 Paring down the 'cheekbone' with the spoon gouge

carve the fronts of the ears so that they angle back at each side. If you cut downwards from the tips of the ears, towards the line and sawcut at the base of the ears, you will be cutting with the grain and the wood will cut away cleanly. Shape the ears at the sides so that they curve in to meet the glue line. Then, cutting up towards the base of the ears, remove the corners and round over at each side of the forehead. Cut

away the corners for the nostrils, which angle back at each side, and pencil in the shape of the nostrils. Cut back all round the nostrils: above them the corners are rounded up to the eye, rounding more near the nostril than near the eye, so that when viewed from the front it tapers from the widest part at the eyebrow down to the narrowest part near the mouth, with just the nostrils sticking out.

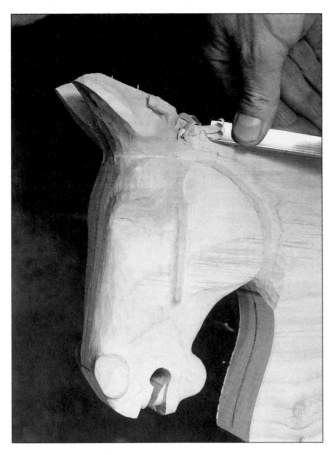

Plate 6.10 Shaping top of neck and ears.
The head is nearing completion — note the teeth

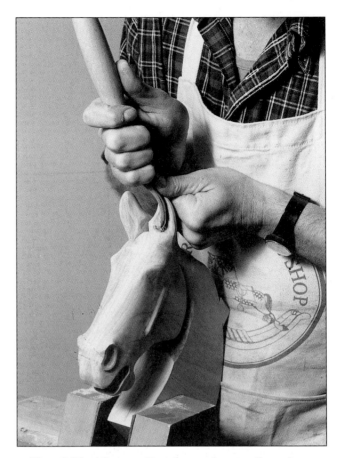

Plate 6.11 After sanding down, the nostrils and ears
are hollowed out

Turn the head on one side and cramp it to the bench. Pare back the area above the eye until it meets the glue line at the top of the cheek, and pare back the 'cheekbone' so that it is proud of the surrounding wood by only about ⅛in (3mm). So far, we have used only the 1in (25mm) shallow gouge. Now take up the ⁵/₁₆in (8mm) straight chisel and make a series of cuts at right angles into the wood along the curved line of the cheek, from the base of the ear round to the neck. Then use the 1in (25mm) shallow gouge again to cut the waste from outside this line, leaving the cheek proud of the neck by about ⅛in (3mm) near the top, ⅜in (10mm) at the lower end of the cheek. With the No 5 gouge carve back below the line that marks the lower part of the cheek, and carry on paring down to the mouth and lower jaw. When finished the mouth will be about 1½in (38mm) wide, or slightly less. Use the No 9 deep gouge to carve round the lower jaw and under the cheek, and to cut back the corner of the eye piece where the eye socket will later be positioned. The head should now be taking on a recognisably horselike shape; turn it over and carve the other side to match.

Use the spoon gouge to cut along either side

Plate 6.12 Cramping the neck down on to the upper-
body block

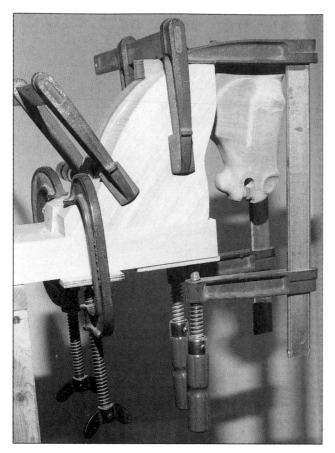

Plate 6.13 Cramping on the neck-muscle blocks

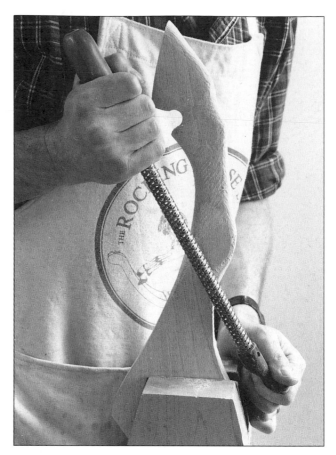

Plate 6.14 Using a round Surform to shape a leg

of the cheekbone so that it runs smoothly into the surrounding wood, and the straight chisel to carefully carve away around the mouth to reveal the teeth. The tops of the ears are shaped with the No 5 gouge, and when you have achieved a pleasing overall appearance, the head can be sanded smooth with 120-grit abrasive. Finally, use the spoon gouge to slightly hollow the insides of the ears and nostrils, and the head is finished, as far as it needs to be at this stage.

Plane the bottom of the neck flat and square. It can now be dowel pegged and glued down to the upper-body block. Make sure it is positioned centrally and use the cramping noggin on the neck when cramping together. Two fluted-dowel pegs are sufficient — for details of the use of dowel pegs and markers, see Appendix 1. When this joint has set, the two neck-muscle blocks can be glued on, one each side. There is no need to use dowel pegs for these, but before glueing do ensure that the muscle blocks fit neatly to the neck and upper body block by planing off their bottoms.

Rough carving and glueing the legs

Now you can rough carve the lower parts of the legs. It is easier to do this before assembly, and I find the simplest way is to use a rasp or Surform

Plate 6.15 The legs are glued and screwed to the lower-body block

to round over the corners. They should be slightly thinner above the fetlocks, but leave the bottoms of the hooves flat and square. Drill and countersink the legs for the screws that will be used to fix them to the lower-body block: 8 x $1\frac{1}{2}$in No 10 countersunk woodscrews will be needed for this, 2 for each leg. The legs are glued and screwed on to the notches bandsawn from each corner of the lower-body block; true up the surfaces to be joined by planing to ensure a good joint before glueing them.

The leg-muscle blocks are glued on over the

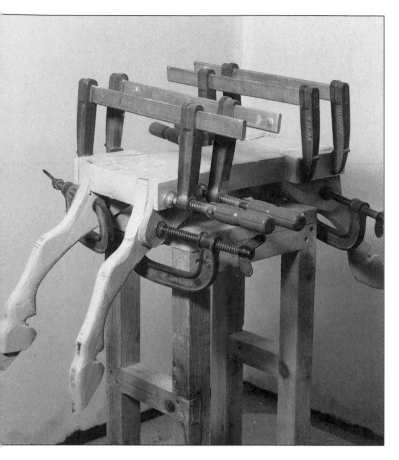

Plate 6.16 Cramps hold legs and leg muscle blocks in position on the lower-body block, until the glue sets

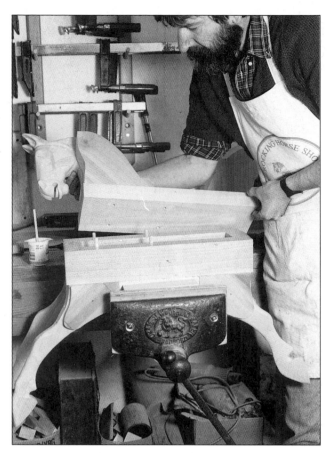

Plate 6.17 The middle-body blocks have been fixed on and now the upper-body block is glued on. The dowel pegs are placed near the inside edges of the middle-body blocks

tops of the legs, and will conceal the leg-fixing screws. Again, make sure that they will be a good fit before glueing. Use a 4in (100mm) G-cramp to cramp each one to its leg, and sliding F-cramps across the tops in conjunction with the waste pieces sawn from each corner of the lower-body block. To prevent the leg-muscle blocks from sliding about while you are cramping them it helps if you nail them on — leave the nailhead proud so that it can be removed later and the nail hole filled. After fixing the legs to the lower-body block the hooves should be the same distance apart front and rear — but do not worry if they are not; this will not affect the ability of the horse to rock. Nor does it matter if the hooves do not stand four-square on a flat surface — they rarely do, and this will be easily corrected later, during hoof notching. You may wonder why the configuration of the legs is such that the horse is tilted up slightly at the front — it is to give the finished horse a slightly prancing appearance.

Glueing-up the rest of the horse
The legs and leg-muscle blocks are glued on so

that their tops are flush with, or slightly proud of, the top of the lower-body block, which can now be planed flat to receive the middle-body blocks. You may need to plane a little from the inside of the middle-body-block sides to let them fit neatly to the ends. Even so the middle-body block sides will overhang the lower-body block by about ¼in (6mm) at each side — this is to allow for the swell of the horse's belly. Place the middle-body blocks on the lower-body block and pencil mark their positions so that you can replace them precisely, and drill for the fluted-dowel pegs. Use three dowel pegs each side and avoid drilling into the leg-fixing screws. There is no need for dowels in the end blocks. If you have enough cramps you will be able to glue and cramp up all the middle-body blocks at the same time.

The last operation in the assembly is to glue and dowel peg the upper-body block (with head and neck attached) to the middle-body blocks (with lower body and legs attached). Again, make sure they fit true before glueing, and use four dowel pegs. Before you glue up, you may like to put a message for posterity into the cavity

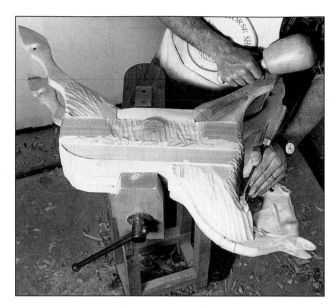

*Plate 6.18 Rough carving the neck with a mallet
and the largest gouge*

*Plate 6.19 Shaping between the front legs
with mallet and gouge, and ...*

in the middle. Some makers put in a 'time cap-sule' with family photographs, newspapers and messages to the future which, of course, if you have built your horse well, you may expect will never be read.

Carving the body and the neck

Pencil in a centre line along the horse's back and down the rear end, and down the chest, to help you to keep it symmetrical. For the rough carving of the body and neck, use the large deep alongee gouge and, if you have one, a drawknife. Put the horse on its side and start by removing the top corners from the neck-muscle blocks at each side. The neck tapers from base to top and at the top will be rounded over. Avoid making the top of the neck too narrow and pointed. Carve off any bits of the leg-muscle blocks that jut out, and cut them back so that they taper down and merge into the legs. Pencil in the curve of the rump and saw off the triangular waste piece. Also saw off the cramping noggin on the neck.

Before you start to round the body, and it becomes more awkward to hold securely, turn the horse upside down so that you can get at the areas between the legs. With the alongee gouge, and a Surform or rasp, round off the insides of the legs so that they run smoothly into the lower-body block. At the front the lower-body block is shaped to leave a bulge in the middle, while at the rear a 'valley' between the legs curves up towards the tail. Rocking-horses do not normally have any carved details between the rear legs since they are presumably all geldings.

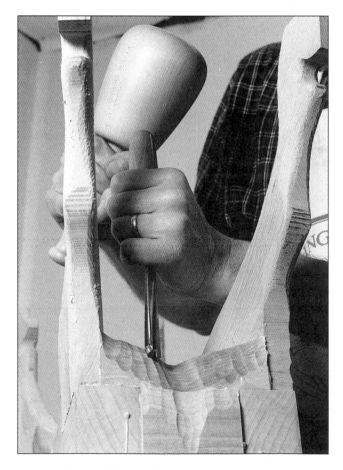

Plate 6.20 ... hollowing between rear legs

Plate 6.21 Using a drawknife on the back; note the gouge marks over the rest of the body

With the horse on its side again, pencil a cross near the centre of the middle block to indicate the highest point of the swell of the belly. Viewed from above, three areas of the body will remain wide: below the neck, at the rump and at the middle of the body. Between these areas — that is, from behind the front leg round to the base of the neck, and in front of the rear leg round to where the saddle block will be placed — the body is shaped thinner. The body is well rounded over the rump and in the middle, where the saddle will fit, and rounded along the lower edges also, though to a lesser extent; the actual underneath of the body remains flat.

Carving is three-dimensional; bear in mind as you carve that any wood you remove from one area will alter the appearance when viewed from any other angle. So keep altering your angle of view to see how the shape is changing. The most common fault of novice carvers is their failure to remove enough wood, to be too tentative, which leaves parts of the horse still looking rather square and box-like. There are no corners on a horse; the shaping on the body and neck should produce slow gentle curves that invite people to run their hands over them.

The shoulders are rounded, but left proud of the area above them, which is cut back towards

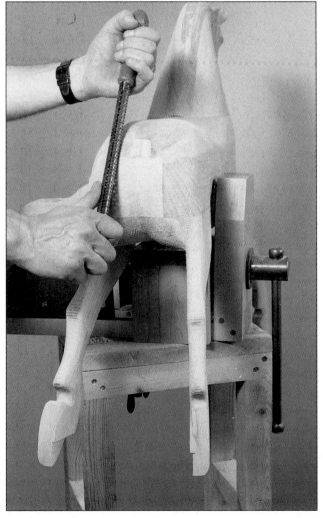

Plate 6.22 Using a round Surform to remove gouge marks and shape the rump

61

Plate 6.23 Detail of the finished Small horse after painting and tacking up

Plate 6.24 The half-round Surform is used to smooth the slow curves of the neck and body

the neck. Below the shoulders the corners of the middle-body blocks are rounded in towards the chest. The chest is one of the more difficult areas to carve, since you have to contend with carving across the end grain of the body blocks towards the middle. The chest finishes up concave in the middle, above the bulge at the centre of the lower-body block. The shape of the base of the neck at the glue line where it joins the upper-body block is that of an almost-pointed egg — 'little end' towards the rear. Keep carving a little from each side in turn so that the shape remains symmetrical about the centre line of the horse's body.

The deep alongee gouge leaves marked ripples, the high points of which you can remove with the shallower 1in (25mm) gouge and Surform or rasp. Surforms are particularly useful for achieving smooth curves, but if you use a round one you will have to keep tapping the bits out of it, or else it will become clogged. You may also find a spokeshave useful for smoothing the curves of the rump and neck. Each maker's horse comes out a little different from every other; carve until you feel you want to go no further, and then stop.

Sanding down

Once you are pleased with the overall shape, you can begin to rub down the surface with abrasive papers. Drum sanding attachments for your electric drill, and pad sanders, will be useful, but there will be a lot of areas where the contours just have to be sanded by hand. Sand with a fairly coarse paper, 80 or 100 grit. If you are going to gesso and paint there is no need for a super-smooth surface, and the rough sanding will provide a key. But if you intend going for a natural-wood finish which will be clear varnished or lacquered, then you will need to sand down with finer and finer papers — 120, 180, 240, and 360 grit — to remove all the blemishes and scratchmarks. Drill a ³/₄in (19mm)-diameter hole for the tail — this hole can go right into the hollow middle of the horse. Now you can think about fitting the glass eyes, and painting and finishing your horse; for details of these techniques, turn to Chapter 10.

CHAPTER 7

HOOF NOTCHES AND SWING-IRON STANDS

All rocking-horses made for mounting on swing-iron stands have their hooves notched so that they fit neatly over the hoof rails of the stand, to which they are secured. The method of marking out the notches, which also takes care of any inequality in the length of the legs, is as follows.

HOW TO MARK AND CUT HOOF NOTCHES

Place the horse on a flat surface and under each hoof tuck a piece of scrap wood about ¼in (6mm) thick. You may well find that the horse leans to one side or wobbles due to unequal leg lengths. If so, tuck further pieces of scrap wood under the hooves until it stands upright and

without wobbling. Take two lengths of ¾in x 1¾in (19mm x 45mm) timber to use as temporary hoof rails. Place them on the flat surface against the inside of the hooves and use a pencil and a pair of compasses open to about ⅜in (9mm) for the Swinger, Little Red Rocker and Small carved horse, ½in (13mm) for Medium or Large horses, to mark and scribe for the hoof notches.

Carefully saw out the hoof notches and drill each hoof for the bolts or woodscrews that will hold the horse on to the hoof rails. Smaller horses can be secured to the hoof rails with either No 8 x 1¼in (32mm) woodscrews or ³⁄₁₆in (5mm) bolts and nuts, but for the Medium or Large rocking-horses use ¼in (6mm) carriage bolts and nuts. Angle the drill downwards so that the holes will not be too close to the top edge of the hoof rails. Then

Fig 1 *Marking out for hoof notches*

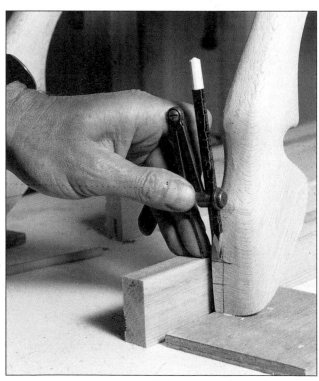

Plate 7.1 Using a pair of compasses to mark out for hoof notches

screw on temporary hoof rails, which serve to prevent the hooves getting chipped as you move the horse around, and also enable you to paint all round the visible part of them.

CUTTING LISTS FOR SWING-IRON STANDS

The swing-iron stands described here have been designed to suit the horses in this book. The small stand fits the Swinger (Chapter 4), the Little Red Rocker (Chapter 5) and the Small carved horse in Chapter 6. The medium and large stands suit the Medium and Large horses described in Chapter 9. The construction method is similar for each of the three sizes. They may be made from pine, or a hardwood such as oak or maple. Prepare your timber according to the appropriate cutting list below; they are the actual finished dimensions required after planing and cutting exactly to length (though timber for posts can be rough sawn to size for turning):

Cutting list: *Small Stand for the Swinger, the Little Red Rocker and the Small Carved Horse*

	Thickness x width x length			Thickness x width x length		
	Inches			Millimetres		
Top rail	¾	x 2¾	x 34	19	x 70	x 864
Bottom rail	¾	x 3¾	x 42	19	x 95	x 1,066
Cross-pieces (x 2)	¾	x 3¾	x 16	19	x 95	x 406
End-pieces (x 2)	¾	x 1¾	x 3½	19	x 45	x 89
Posts (x 2)	2¾	x 2¾	x 16	70	x 70	x 406
Hoof rails (x 2)	¾	x 1¾	x 34	19	x 45	x 864

Cutting list: *Medium Stand for the Medium Carved Horse*

	Thickness x width x length			Thickness x width x length		
	Inches			Millimetres		
Top rail	⅞	x 3¾	x 46	21	x 95	x 1,168
Bottom rail	1¼	x 5¾	x 53	32	x 146	x 1,346
Cross-pieces (x 2)	1¼	x 5¾	x 18	32	x 146	x 457
End-pieces (x 2)	1¼	x 1¾	x 5½	32	x 45	x 140
Posts (x 2)	3	x 3	x 20	75	x 75	x 508
Hoof rails (x 2)	⅞	x 1¾	x 42	21	x 45	x 1,067

Cutting list: *Large Stand for the Large Carved Horse*

	Thickness x width x length			Thickness x width x length		
	Inches			Millimetres		
Top rail	⅞	x 3¾	x 52	21	x 95	x 1,321
Bottom rail	1¼	x 5¾	x 60	32	x 146	x 1,524
Cross-pieces (x 2)	1¼	x 5¾	x 21	32	x 146	x 533
End-pieces (x 2)	1¼	x 1¾	x 5½	32	x 45	x 140
Posts (x 2)	4	x 4	x 23½	100	x 100	x 600
Hoof rails (x 2)	⅞	x 2¾	x 52½	21	x 70	x 1,334

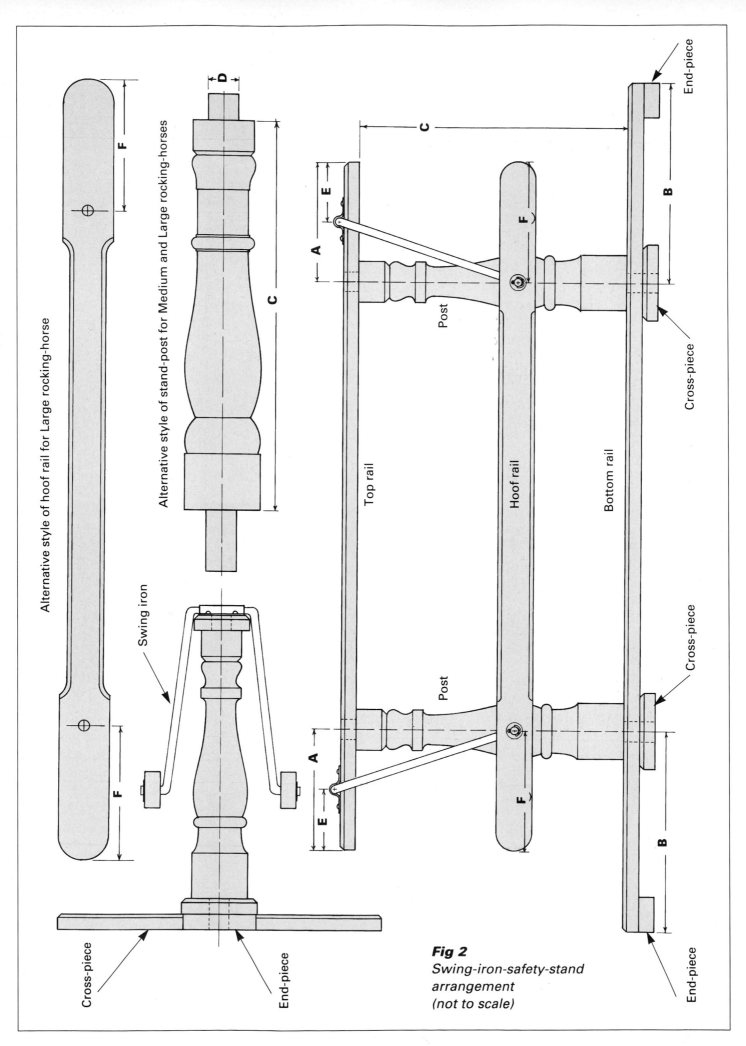

Alternative style of hoof rail for Large rocking-horse

Alternative style of stand-post for Medium and Large rocking-horses

D

F

C

Swing iron

F

Cross-piece

End-piece

C

E

A

Post

Top rail

Hoof rail

Bottom rail

F

Post

A

E

F

B

End-piece

B

Cross-piece

Cross-piece

End-piece

Fig 2
*Swing-iron-safety-stand
arrangement
(not to scale)*

66

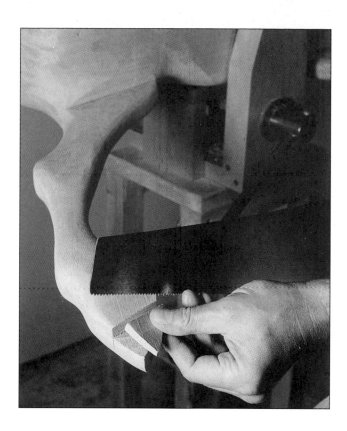

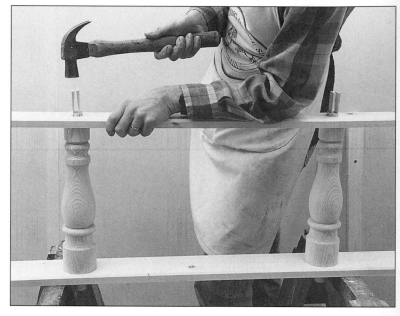

Plate 7.3 Assembling a small pine stand.
Hammer the wedges in tight

Plate 7.2 Sawing out a hoof notch

The following table shows the measurements indicated on Fig 2:

	Stand for Swinger, Little Red Rocker and Small Carved Horse	Stand for Medium Carved Horse	Stand for Large Carved Horse
A Post centres, from ends of top rail	6in (152mm)	7½in (190mm)	8in (203mm)
B Post centres, from ends of bottom rail	10in (254mm)	11in (279mm)	12in (305mm)
C Length of post between rails	13in (330mm)	15½in (394mm)	19in (483mm)
D Diameter of post pegs, and post-peg holes	1in (25mm)	1⅜in (35mm)	1⅜in (35mm)
E Swing iron, from ends of top rail	3in (76mm)	3in (76mm)	3in (76mm)
F Swing-iron holes, from ends of hoof rails	6in (152mm)	6in (152mm)	7¼in (184mm)

THE CONSTRUCTION OF SWING-IRON STANDS

Note that the top rail and the hoof rails are rounded at the ends. The top and bottom rails and the cross-pieces are chamfered at 45° all around their top edges. The hoof rails may also be chamfered, but these chamfers should be stopped about 1½in (38mm) before the swing-iron holes. Fig 2 also shows an alternative style of hoof rail which you may like to use with the large stand.

The posts are normally turned, with pegs or spigots which fit through appropriate-sized holes in the top and bottom rails. The lower-end post peg also passes through a hole drilled in the centre of the cross-piece. The cross-and end-pieces are glued and screwed on to the bottom rail; see Fig 3. The posts are secured by glueing and driving wooden wedges into a couple of saw cuts across the pegs. Do ensure that the wedges are placed at right angles to the direction of grain of the surrounding timber. Fig 2 shows two traditional styles of stand-posts, and Fig 4 shows some alternatives. If you do not have a lathe, posts can be made up from square- or rectangular-section timber, appropriately jointed into the top and bottom rails (Fig 4D).

The swing irons are made from bright mild-steel rod: ⅜in (10mm) diameter for the Swinger, Little Red Rocker and Small horses; ⁷⁄₁₆in (11mm) diameter for the Medium and

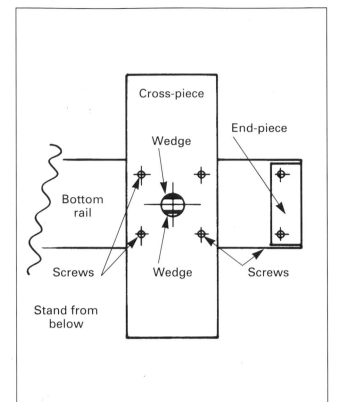

Plate 7.4 The end-pieces and cross-pieces are glued and screwed on to the bottom rail before hammering home the wedges — note the wedges are at right-angles to the direction of grain of the cross-piece

Fig 3 *Detail showing fixing of cross-pieces to bottom rail (not to scale)*

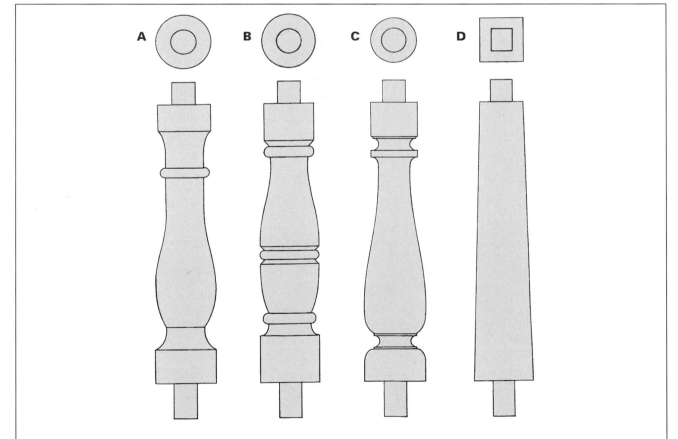

Fig 4 *Alternative styles of stand post (not to scale). A, B and C are turned, D is tapered square section with square tenons top and bottom*

Plate 7.5 All the metalwork: steel swing irons, brass brackets, and bowler hats, steel bearing strips and fixing bolts, screws, washers and pins

Plate 7.6 Saw off the waste ends of the pegs. A piece of thin card cut and held as shown will prevent the saw's teeth damaging the top rail

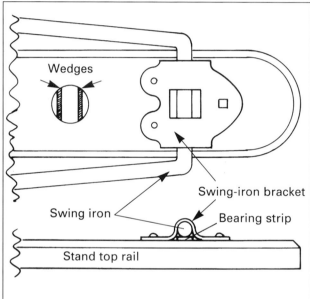

Fig 5 Detail showing arrangement of swing-iron bracket (not to scale)

Labels: Wedges, Swing-iron bracket, Swing iron, Bearing strip, Stand top rail

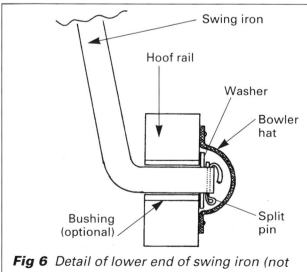

Fig 6 Detail of lower end of swing iron (not to scale)

Labels: Swing iron, Hoof rail, Washer, Bowler hat, Bushing (optional), Split pin

Plate 7.7 Brass bracket on a small stand

Large horses. They should be as long as possible in order to give a good rocking action, while allowing sufficient clearance over the top rail so that a child could not get his or her fingers trapped. That is 9¼in (235mm) long for the Swinger, Little Red Rocker and Small horse, 12½in (318mm) long for the Medium, and 14½in (368mm) long for the Large horse. The lower ends pass through holes in the hoof rails which should be drilled fractionally larger than the diameter of the swing irons so that they will pivot freely. It is really not necessary to bush these holes since in normal use they suffer surprisingly little wear, even over many years. However, if we are making a horse for a school or hospital, where it is likely to come in for exceptionally hard usage, then we do insert bushes, which we cut from copper pipe.

It will almost certainly be the case that the distance between the hoofs of your horse will be different front and back, but it is important that the swing irons are adjusted to fit properly. They need to be pushed closer together or pulled further apart so that when the horse is lifted on to its rails the ends of the irons protrude just far enough to accommodate the securing washers and split pins. The horse's legs should not be put under any strain by ill-fitting swing irons. The steel swing irons can then be primed and painted. See Appendix 2 for details of suppliers of rocking-horse fittings.

A strip of ½in (12mm)-wide steel will be screwed on to the top rail of the stand for the swing iron to bear upon. The swing iron is held in position on the top rail by steel or polished-brass brackets, secured with ¼in (6mm)-diameter carriage bolts (and screws in the case of the small brackets). Mark the positions of the bearing strips and brackets and drill the bolt holes, but before assembling the metalwork give the stand and hoof rails a final sand-down. Stands are usually varnished, and may be stained as well, or they may be primed and painted, as you prefer. When you fit the metal-work, add a dab of grease under the brackets and to the lower ends of the swing irons. Screw on four brass 'bowler hats' to cover the ends of the swing irons. These finish off the stand neat-ly, and it is now time to lift on the horse.

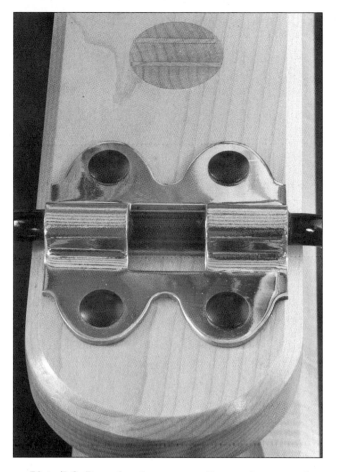

Plate 7.9 Brass bracket on a medium or large stand

Plate 7.8 A brass 'bowler hat' screwed to the hoof rail covers the lower end of the swing iron

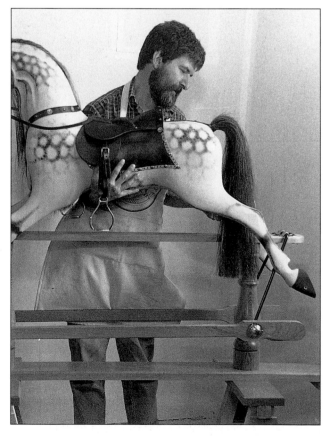

Plate 7.10 The stand is finished and the horse, in this case a large one, is lifted on

CHAPTER 8
A SMALL TRADITIONAL CARVED ROCKING-HORSE
on Bow Rockers

Bow-shaped rockers were used to make toy horses rock long before the swing-iron safety stand was developed, and many people still regard bows as the real and 'proper' form of the rocking-horse. They can indeed look superb, and have an excellent rocking action that will delight their riders. But they do have disadvantages. A horse on bows is much longer and therefore takes up more space than a horse of similar size mounted on a safety stand. It tends to move about on the floor as it is ridden, bumping into walls and furniture. And if a child stands too close whilst the horse is being ridden, there is the danger of it rocking over small toes. For these reasons we recommend bow rockers be used only for small rocking-horses.

The horse itself is constructed in exactly the same manner as the Small horse in Chapter 6. The only difference lies in the configuration of the legs. Use the cutting list on page 50 when preparing the timber for all the parts of this horse — with the exception of the legs and leg-muscle blocks which are listed below.

Because this horse is to be mounted on bow rockers the legs are more stretched out to front and rear than for the stand-mounted horse, but the jointing of the legs to the lower-body block is the same. (The stand-mounted horse has its legs in a more 'upright' stance in order to ensure that there is sufficient room between the legs to accommodate the swing irons.) All the shaping is accomplished in the same manner as for the stand-mounted horse described in Chapter 6, and all the instructions given for that horse concerning assembly and carving apply to this one.

MAKING BOW ROCKERS

Bow rockers are best made from ash, for its springy quality, but oak, beech or other hardwood may also be used. Each side of the bow is made from two pieces joined at the centre to each side of a rectangular frame around which the rockers are assembled. The frame sides and ends are cut from the same piece of timber as the bows. Prepare the timber as follows:

Cutting list

	Thickness x width x length			Thickness x width x length		
	Inches			**Millimetres**		
Legs (all four)	$\frac{7}{8}$ x $5\frac{3}{4}$ x	54		22 x 146	x 1,372
Leg-muscle blocks (all)	$\frac{3}{8}$ x $5\frac{3}{4}$ x	28		10 x 146	x 711
Bow rockers and frame (x 2)	$\frac{3}{4}$ x $6\frac{1}{4}$ x	65		19 x 159	x 1,651
Slatted platform (x 6)	$\frac{5}{8}$ x $1\frac{3}{4}$ x	$12\frac{1}{2}$		16 x 45	x 318
End-pieces (x 2)	$1\frac{3}{4}$ x $1\frac{3}{4}$ x	6		45 x 45	x 152

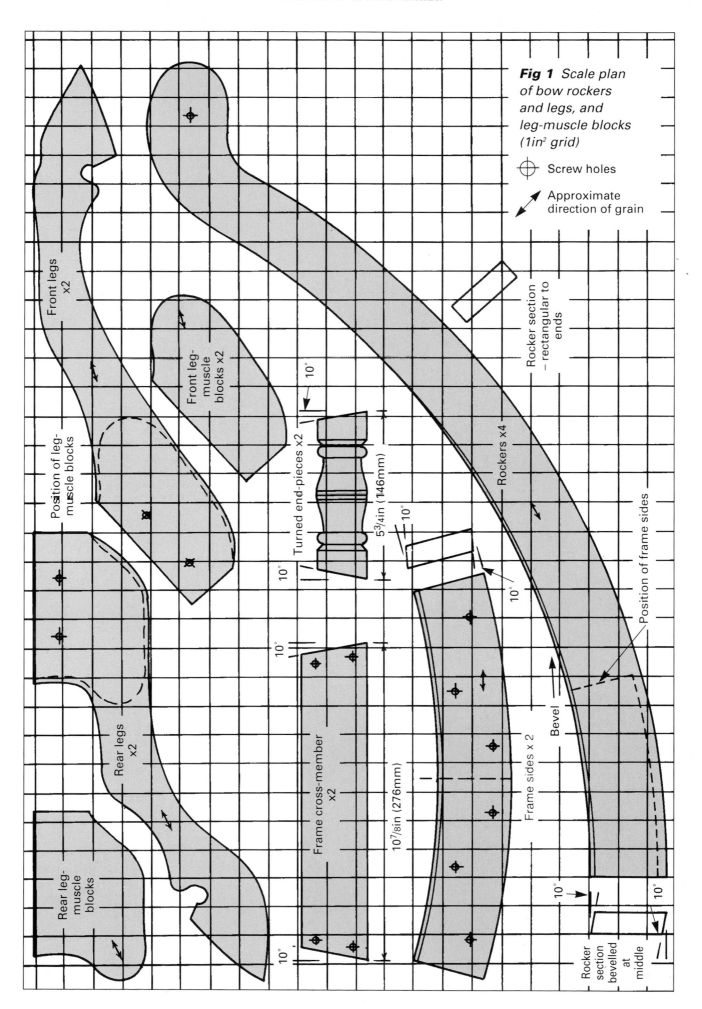

Fig 1 Scale plan of bow rockers and legs, and leg-muscle blocks (1in² grid)

⊕ Screw holes

↗ Approximate direction of grain

Front legs x2

Front leg-muscle blocks x2

Position of leg-muscle blocks

Rear legs x2

Rear leg-muscle blocks

Turned end-pieces x2

5³/4in (146mm)

10°

10°

10°

Frame cross-member x2

10⁷/8in (276mm)

10°

10°

Rocker section – rectangular to ends

Rockers x4

Position of frame sides

Bevel

Frame sides x 2

10°

10°

10°

Rocker section bevelled at middle

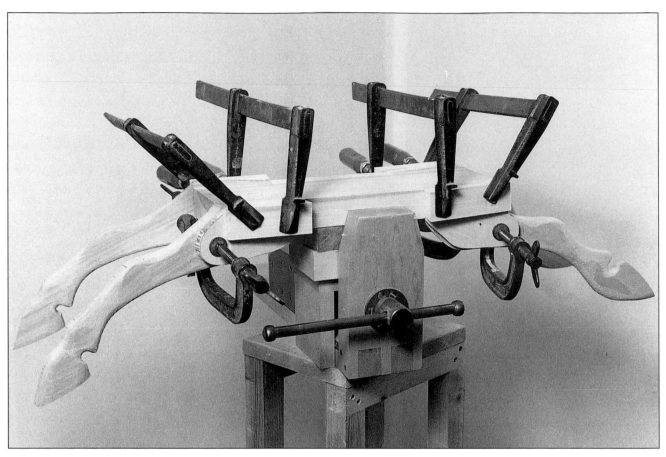

Plate 8.1 Legs and leg-muscle blocks glued and cramped on to the lower-body block. The configuration of the legs is the only difference between this one and the Small horse made for swing-iron-stand mounting

Plate 8.2 The horse at the rough carved stage

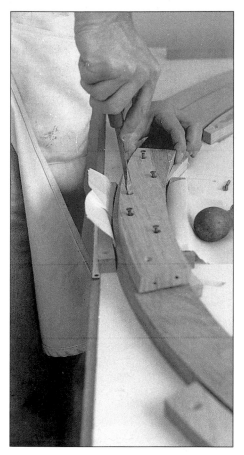

*Plate 8.3 Glueing and screwing
the rocker frame sides to the rockers*

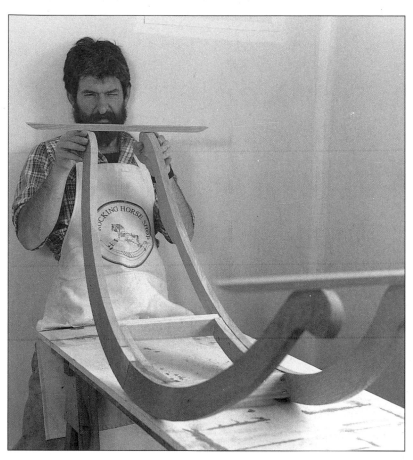

*Plate 8.4 Sighting across two winding sticks to ensure
the rocker assembly is true*

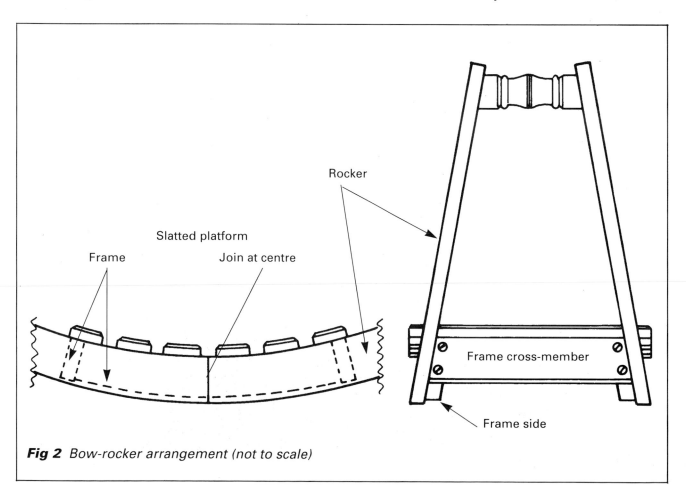

Rocker

Slatted platform

Frame   Join at centre

Frame cross-member

Frame side

Fig 2 *Bow-rocker arrangement (not to scale)*

The width given for the rockers (ie 6¼in or 159mm) is the minimum needed, and if you can obtain wider boards you will be able to economise on the length. In any case, you should position the patterns carefully bearing in mind that the rockers and rocker-frame sides have bevelled edges towards the middle and due allowance must be made for these; so study the drawings before cutting out. Instead of hardwood, some makers use ¾in (19mm) plywood for the rocker sides and frame. In this case it is possible to cut each side of the rocker in one piece and dispense with the joint in the middle, although the wastage will be greater.

The distinctive boat-shaped appearance, in which the rockers are closer together at the ends than in the middle, is formed by angling the two rockers, at 10° from the vertical, towards each other. They are not steamed or bent. The edges of the rockers are bevelled so that they sit flat to the floor underneath and so that the slatted platform will sit flat on top of them, but this bevelling runs out before the ends of the rockers where they become rectangular in section. The two curved frame sides are also bevelled at 10°, top and bottom. If you have a bandsaw on which the table can be tilted to 10° you will be able to bandsaw the bevels. If not, the bevels will have to be cut by hand with a spokeshave, and due allowance should be left for them when cutting out. Take particular care when marking and cutting out the timber that the bevels angle the correct way.

The two pieces that form each side of the bow rocker are simply butted together and secured by glueing and screwing on the frame sides with 1¼in (32mm) No 8 woodscrews. We have made up a jig to help to ensure that the

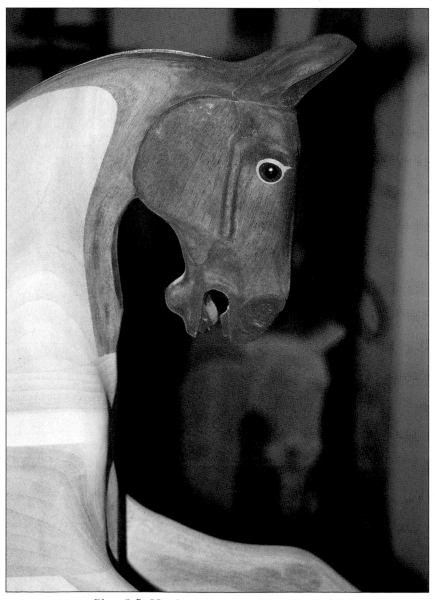

Plate 8.5 Head carving complete and eyes fitted

Plate 8.6 The turned end-pieces and slatted platform have been secured and the horse, which has been sanded smooth, is fitted to the rockers after carefully notching the hooves

Plate 8.7 Finished Small horse on bow rockers

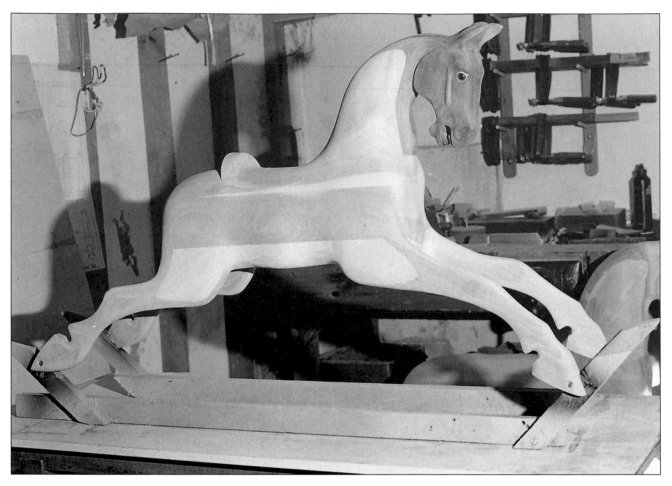

Plate 8.8 The horse is ready for the paint shop — the glass eyes and saddle block have been fitted and it is screwed on to a pair of temporary rails as shown

rockers are assembled correctly. It consists simply of a drawing of the full rocker on a piece of board with scraps of wood screwed on at intervals round the edges, so that the rocker parts can be wedged in position while they are glued and screwed together. It is not really necessary to go to the trouble of making a special assembly jig if you are only making one horse, but you must ensure that the bevels correspond, that the pieces are drawn as close together as possible, and most important, that you get a smooth curve across the joint (or it will click when it rocks). The rocker-frame cross-pieces are glued and screwed on to the ends of the frame sides, thus joining together the two bows which angle in towards each other. Before the glue has dried place a straight 'winding' stick across each end of the bow rockers, then stand back and sight across them. The winding sticks should be parallel — if not, pull at the rockers until they are and then let the glue dry.

The ends of the rockers are joined together with the two end-pieces. These are normally turned to the pattern shown, but may be square or octagonal if you do not have a lathe. Saw off

Plate 8.9 Detail showing how notched hooves fit over rockers

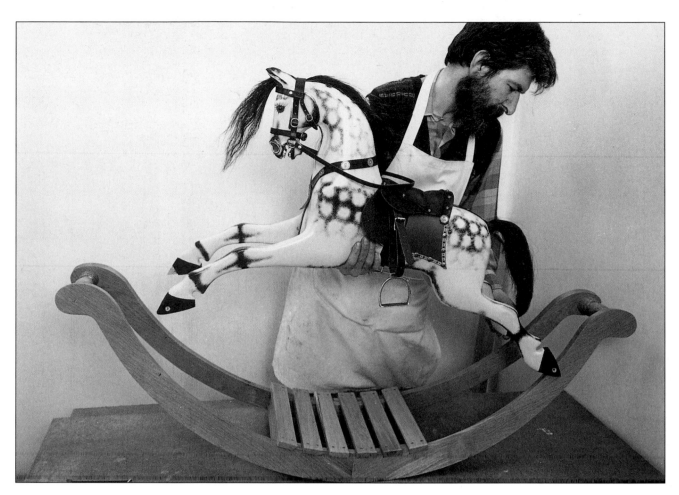

Plate 8.10 Lifting the finished horse on to its rockers.
A hacksaw will be used to trim off the securing bolts

the ends at 10° angles. The easiest way of fixing them in place is to drill a $^3/_{16}$in (5mm) hole through each rocker end, prick-mark the centres of the end-pieces, spread glue on them and screw in position with $1^1/_2$in (32mm) No 8 woodscrews. You may need to cramp them also. When the glue has set remove the screws and enlarge the holes to $^3/_8$in (9mm) — let the drill penetrate at least an inch (25mm) into the end-piece. Put some glue into the holes and drive in $^3/_8$in (9mm)-diameter dowel pegs. Saw off the waste ends of the dowel pegs and sand smooth. The tops of the six pieces for the slatted platform are chamfered all round and fixed on to the rockers at each side with 1in (25mm) No 6 brass woodscrews. Make sure that they overhang equally at each side and space them apart evenly, by eye.

FITTING THE HORSE TO THE ROCKERS

Before giving the rockers a final sand-down and varnishing, the hoof notches can be marked and cut ready for the horse to be fitted on. Wedge some scrap wood under the rockers to stop them moving and lift the horse on to the rockers so that each hoof rests on the outer edge of the rockers and the horse is not tilting to one side. It is best to have some help to position the horse, in case it slips and falls off. By carefully marking and cutting away a little at the inside of each hoof with saw and chisel, the hooves are notched so that they drop down to overlap the rockers by about an inch (25mm).

Notching the hooves for fixing to the bow rockers is probably the trickiest part of making this horse, because of the odd angles involved. You may well have to lift the horse on and off several times before getting the notches to fit just right, and sometimes it is necessary to glue a packing piece on to the inside of the hooves. Once the horse fits neatly on the rockers you can drill for the bolt holes. Although only four $^3/_{16}$in (5mm) bolts and nuts are used to secure the horse to its rockers, experience has shown that this is sufficiently strong and effective. Remove from the rockers and screw a scrap of wood on to each hoof, to prevent them from being chipped, and turn to Chapter 10 for details of finishing and painting the horse.

CHAPTER 9
MEDIUM AND LARGE TRADITIONAL CARVED ROCKING-HORSES

Whilst the Small rocking-horse described in Chapter 6 is an excellent woodworking project, and fine for the smaller child, the Medium-size horse is considerably bigger and will be good for riders up to the age of eight or more. In fact, it will easily take even an adult's weight; my wife used to ride our own Medium-size rocking-horse with the children, when they were babies. The Medium is by far the most popular size. The Large rocking-horse is bigger again, and is for the more ambitious woodworker who wants to make the biggest and, potentially, the finest of rocking-horses.

CONSTRUCTION REQUIREMENTS

The basic method of making both the Medium and Large horses is broadly similar to that for the Small horse, so you should read Chapter 6 thoroughly before starting one of these. But they are not just scaled-up versions of the small design, and they involve significant variations in, and additions to, the construction method and the carving of detail.

These variations are intended to enhance the designs and, I hope, will add interest to the projects, because they mean that the three horses are very different from each other in configuration and character, as well as in actual size. There are three main differences in the construction.

First, the legs of the Medium and Large horses are jointed into the lower-body block at different angles. As you can see from Figs 1 and 2, where the lower-body block is notched out at each corner, the angle is 8° from the vertical for

body has not been devised by computer-aided design, nor by mathematical formulae, but by experience. Not only does it work, it looks good, and makes for very strong joints and, although it sounds complicated, it is in practice relatively easy to do.

Second, the head and the neck are cut from separate pieces of timber. The head is bevelled where it is jointed to the neck, which has the effect of slightly angling the head off to one side. This angling of the head gives the horse the appearance of turning its head a little — a charming touch of life lacking in rocking-horses built all in a straight line, and well worth the small extra effort.

Third, the Medium and Large horses both have two neck-muscle blocks glued either side of the neck rather than just the one for the Small horse. When the neck is fixed down on to the upper-body block it is angled slightly to one side, thus accentuating the angling of the head mentioned above, and further enhancing the

Plate 9.1 Carving the slight hollow in the chest, one of the more awkward places to carve because of the grain running in different directions

Cutting List: *Medium Carved Rocking-Horse*

	Thickness x width x length			Thickness x width x length		
	Inches			**Millimetres**		
Head	$2^3/_4$ x 7	x	$10^1/_2$	70 x 178	x	267
Neck	$2^3/_4$ x $8^3/_4$	x	11	70 x 222	x	279
Ear and eye pieces (both)	$^1/_2$ x $3^3/_4$	x	14	13 x 95	x	356
1st Neck-muscle blocks (both)	$1^3/_4$ x $8^3/_4$	x	26	45 x 222	x	660
2nd Neck-muscle blocks (both)	$1^1/_4$ x $8^3/_4$	x	16	32 x 222	x	406
Lower-body block	$2^3/_4$ x $8^3/_4$	x	24	70 x 222	x	610
Middle-body block (sides **x** 2)	$2^3/_4$ x $3^3/_4$	x	24	70 x 95	x	610
Middle-body block (ends **x** 2)	$2^3/_4$ x $3^3/_4$	x	$3^1/_2$	70 x 95	x	90
Upper-body block	$1^3/_4$ x $8^3/_4$	x	24	45 x 222	x	610
Legs (all four)	$1^1/_4$ x $7^3/_4$	x	62	32 x 197	x	1,574
Leg-muscle blocks (all four)	$^1/_2$ x $7^3/_4$	x	29	13 x 197	x	737
Saddle block	$^7/_8$ x 2	x	7	22 x 50	x	178

Cutting list: *Large Carved Rocking-Horse*

	Thickness x width x length			Thickness x width x length		
	Inches			**Millimetres**		
Head	$2^3/_4$ x $7^3/_4$	x	$12^1/_2$	70 x 197	x	318
Neck	$2^3/_4$ x $9^3/_4$	x	12	70 x 248	x	305
Ear and eye pieces (both)	$^1/_2$ x $4^1/_2$	x	16	13 x 114	x	406
1st Neck-muscle blocks (both)	$1^3/_4$ x $9^3/_4$	x	30	45 x 248	x	762
2nd Neck-muscle blocks (both)	$1^3/_4$ x $8^3/_4$	x	18	45 x 222	x	457
Lower-body block	$2^3/_4$ x $9^3/_4$	x	$27^3/_4$	70 x 248	x	705
Middle-body block (sides **x** 2)	$2^3/_4$ x $4^3/_4$	x	$27^3/_4$	70 x 121	x	705
Middle-body block (ends **x** 2)	$2^3/_4$ x $4^3/_4$	x	$4^1/_2$	70 x 121	x	114
Upper-body block	$1^3/_4$ x $9^3/_4$	x	$27^3/_4$	45 x 248	x	705
Legs (all four)	$1^3/_8$ x $8^3/_4$	x	76	35 x 222	x	1,930
Leg-muscle blocks (all four)	$^1/_2$ x 8	x	32	13 x 203	x	813
Saddle block	$^7/_8$ x $2^3/_4$	x	8	22 x 70	x	203

CONSTRUCTION METHODS

When bandsawing out the shaped parts, note that you need to allow for the bevels on the straight top edges of the legs and on the head where it is to join to the neck. The head-bevel allowance is about $^1/_2$in (13mm) and I find it easiest to plane this bevel off. The angle of the bevel you make need not be precise, so long as you get a good joint between head and neck. Strengthen the joint with two fluted-dowel pegs and cramp together using the cramping noggin on the neck and the waste piece cut from the front of the head. The ear and eye pieces are glued on at either side and the head is ready to carve. I normally carve the head virtually to completion prior to fixing the neck to the upper-body block since it is easier to turn and work on. Examine the accompanying photographs to see the shapes and contours involved. (Full size plans and a Making Rocking Horses video are available — see Appendix 2.)

The small triangular piece at the base of the neck can be glued on after the neck has been fixed down to the upper-body block. As mentioned above, the neck is fixed down at a slight angle to the body, and this joint is strengthened by three fluted-dowel pegs. The neck-muscle blocks are glued on either side, and you will find that because of the angling of the neck they tend to stick out at what appear to be pecu-

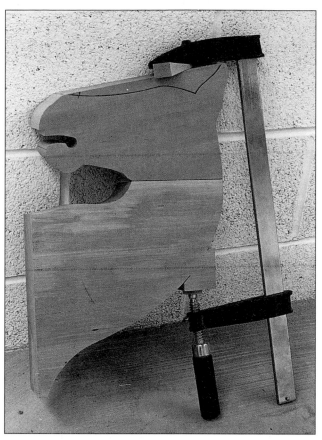

Plate 9.2 Glueing head to neck using waste off-cut at front of head

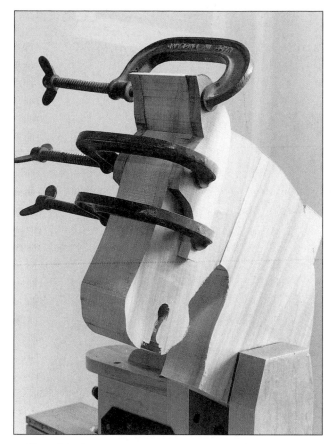

Plate 9.3 This large head has been glued and pegged to the neck, and now the ear and eye pieces are glued on at either side

Plate 9.4 The large head, showing the initial carving of the ears and nostrils

Plate 9.5 The head tapers from eyebrow to mouth, with the nostrils sticking out

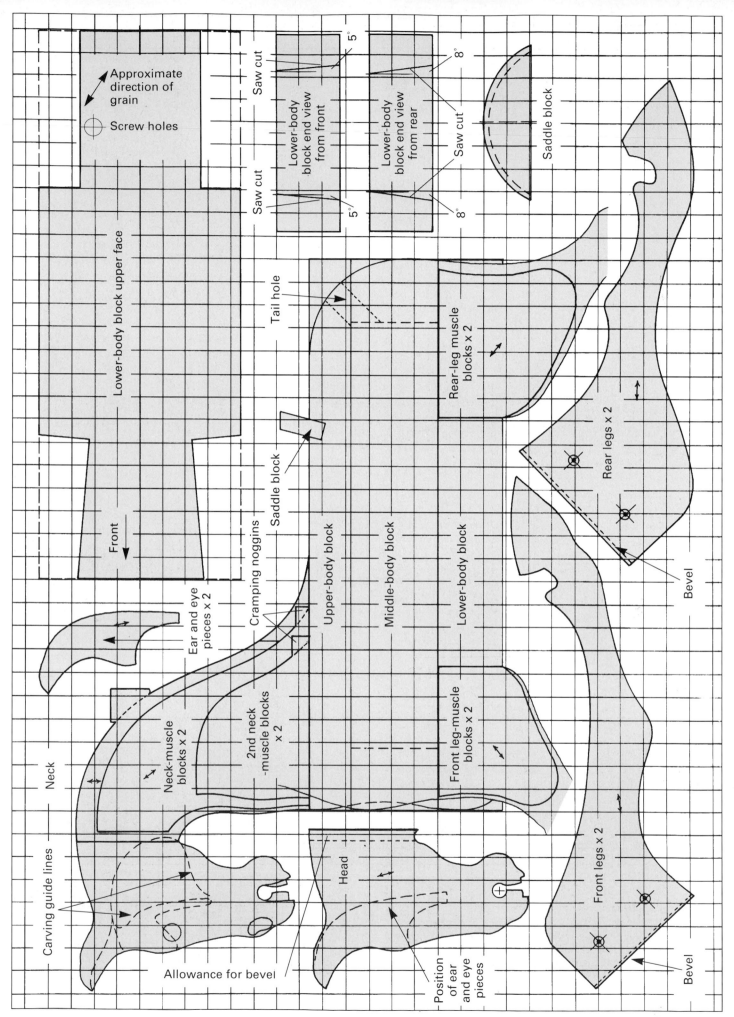

Fig 1 *Scale plan for Medium rocking-horse, showing arrangement of blocks (1in² grid)*

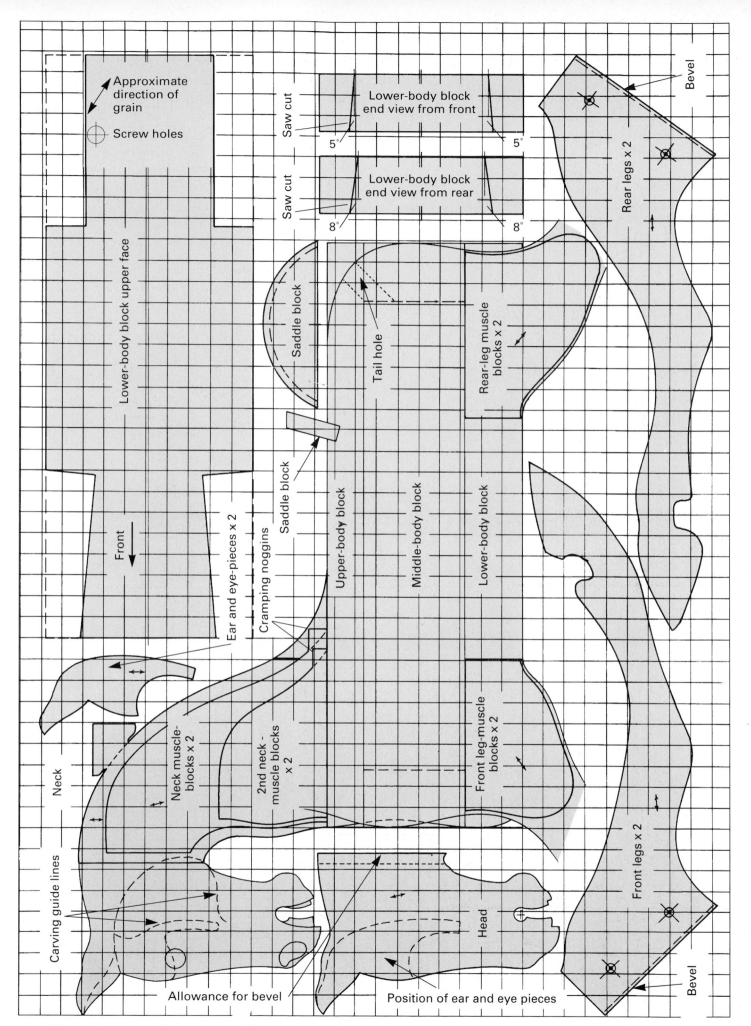

Fig 2 *Scale plan for Large rocking-horse, showing arrangement of blocks (1in² grid)*

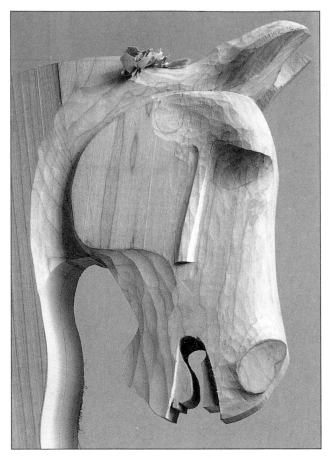

*Plate 9.6 Showing the shape of the cheek and the mouth
cut back for the teeth and tongue*

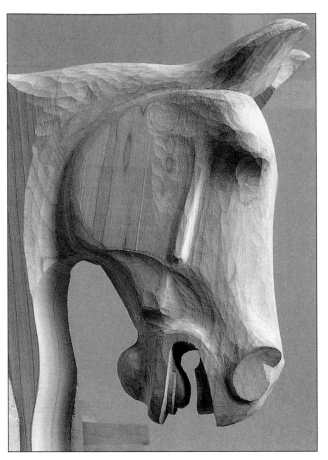

*Plate 9.7 The rough carving of the large head
is almost complete*

*Plates 9.8/9.9 After a thorough sanding down the teeth are defined with V-cuts,
and the ears and nostrils hollowed out*

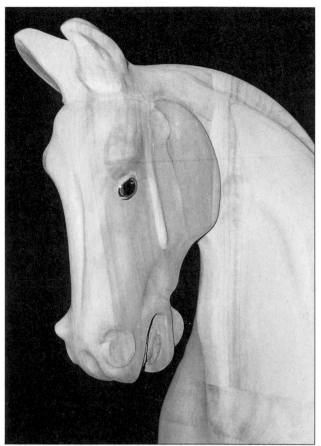

Plate 9.10 Close-up of large head — carving complete and glass eyes fitted

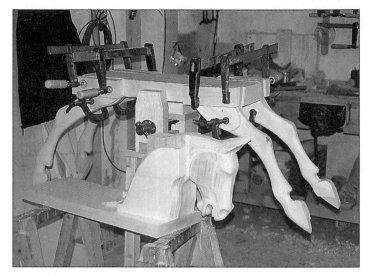

Plate 9.12 Fixing legs and leg-muscle blocks to lower-body block and, in the foreground, the upper-body block with head and first neck-muscle blocks in place

Plate 9.13 Planing the lower-body block flat to receive the middle blocks

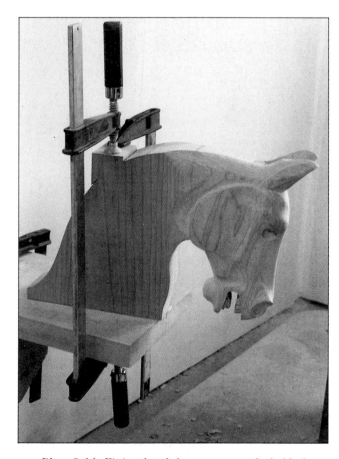

Plate 9.11 Fixing head down to upper-body block

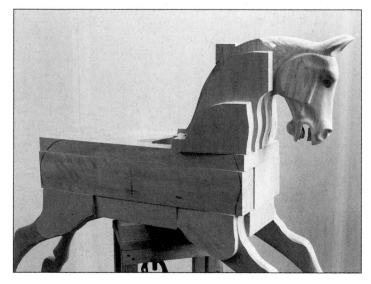

Plate 9.14 The Large horse blocked up ready to start the body and neck carving

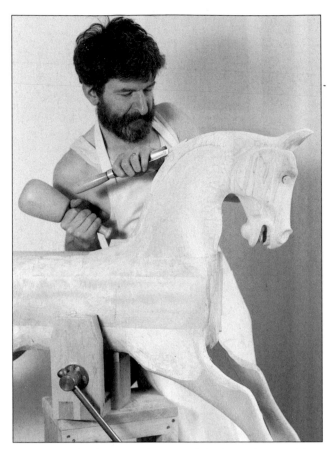

Plate 9.15 Carving the neck of the Large horse with large gouge and mallet — hot work!

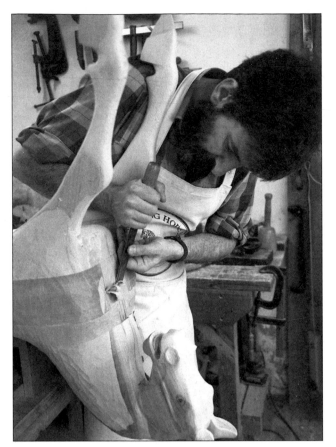

Plate 9.17 Having the horse upside down helps to get a better angle for carving the chest. This is a Medium horse

Plate 9.16 Carving the bulge at the bottom of the chest

liar angles. Do not worry about this, you will lose all these jutting-out bits in the carving.

Notching out the lower-body block at the appropriate angles to receive the legs needs a little thought. Mark out the upper face of the lower-body block as shown on the plan. The saw cuts in from the sides are vertical. If you have a bandsaw with a table that will tilt both ways you only need to tilt the table to the appropriate angle to make the cuts in from the ends. Do

make sure your saw cuts angle the right way (it is easy to get it wrong!) so that the legs will splay out from the body. Keep the pieces cut from each corner; they will help you in cramping on the legs.

If you do not have a tilting-table bandsaw then you need to mark the angles on the ends of the lower-body block as shown on the plan, and saw the notches out by hand. Do not worry if the angles you cut in the lower-body block are not precisely spot-on. If the hoofs do not end up exactly the same distance apart front and back, or if the legs do not stand four-square on a flat surface, these can be corrected for later by adjusting the swing irons and when cutting the hoof notches.

Rough carve the lower parts of the legs. Make sure that the leg joints are good by cleaning up the lower-body-block notches with a smoothing plane. The straight top edges of the legs should be bevelled (5° front, 8° rear), either by handplaning or on the bandsaw. Glue and screw the legs in position so that the tops are slightly proud of the upper face of the lower-body block. Glue on the leg-muscle blocks, which conceal the screws in the legs, and cramp in place. When set, plane the upper face of the

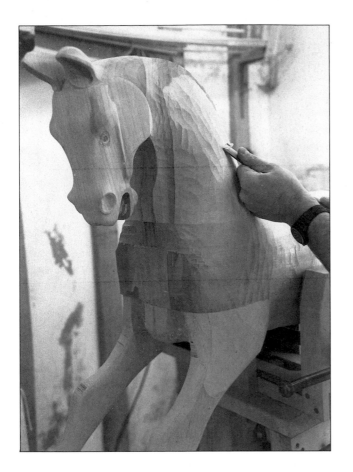

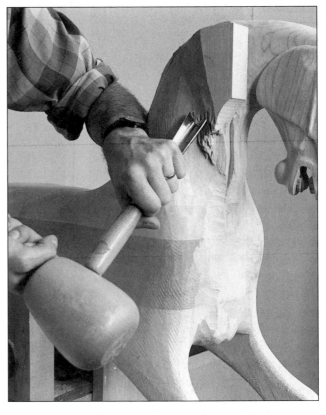

Plates 9.18/9.19 Carving the neck of a Medium horse

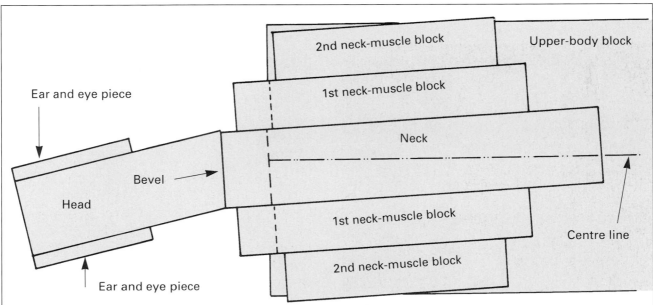

Fig 3 *Showing angling of head to neck, and neck and neck-muscle blocks to upper-body block (not to scale) for Medium and Large horses*

lower-body block flat to receive the middle blocks which are glued in place with three fluted-dowel pegs along each side. Place the dowel pegs towards the inside edge of the middle-body blocks. Insert a message for posterity and glue on the upper-body block, using four fluted-dowel pegs, and you are ready for the body and neck carving.

Carving the body and neck

I mentioned above that it is unnecessary to achieve a high degree of precision when cutting joints, so long as they are good and strong. Similarly carving is not a precise art. People with, for example, an engineering background, who are used to dealing with tolerances in the order of thousandths of an inch, often express

Plate 9.20 *When the carving is complete the horse is thoroughly sanded down*

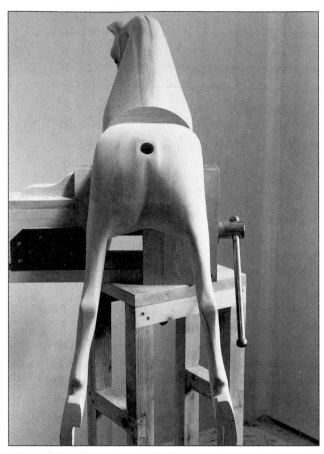

Plate 9.21 *Rear view of the Medium horse showing tail hole and shape of legs. This one already has a saddle block fitted*

Plate 9.22 *Medium head with eye position marked*

Plate 9.23 *Medium head with carving complete and eye in position*

Plate 9.24 Medium horse: body carving almost complete prior to final sanding down

some concern about the relative imprecision of woodcarving. But it is not sensible to aim for 'accuracy' in a job such as this. Do not say to yourself, 'This is going wrong; I must get it correct'. Rather, stand back periodically, look carefully at what you are doing, and say to yourself, 'Can I enhance the shape and form by carving more off here, rounding over more there?'. If you become frustrated with it, if the wished-for shape does not seem to be coming, leave it alone for a while. When you come back to it you may well be able to see your way forward with fresh eyes. It will come good eventually.

When making the Medium or Large rocking-horse you may wish to aim for rather more detail in the carving than was described for the Small horse. You will see from the pictures that a tongue has been carved, and the teeth marked out by V-cuts made with a straight chisel. Some shaping suggests the muscling around the mouth, and neck and crest muscling is carved with a deep gouge. Although the head has been angled off to one side, the neck should be carved so that the base of the neck is central, both at the front where it runs down towards the chest, and at the rear where the saddle will be placed.

As for the Small horse, use the larger gouges and drawknife for roughing out the carving, then the smaller gouges for picking out the details, and finally Surforms or rasp and spokeshave for smoothing off the curves. Drill a 1in (25mm) hole for the tail and give the horse a thorough sanding down. Turn to Chapter 7 for details of hoof notching and stand making, and Chapters 10 and 11 for finishing, painting and tacking up.

CHAPTER 10

FINISHING TOUCHES AND PAINTING CARVED HORSES

FITTING GLASS EYES

With the carving of the horse completed, there are just a few finishing touches to add before you prepare it for painting. Fitting glass eyes will really bring the head to life: use ⁵⁄₈in (16mm)-diameter glass eyes for Small horses, ³⁄₄in (20mm) eyes for Medium horses, and 1in (24mm) eyes for Large horses. They are not always precisely round, and the diameters do tend to vary slightly, but real glass eyes are much better than plastic — they do not scratch so easily and have a real glint to them. They may come attached to thin wires which should be cut off.

Mark the eye positions, taking care to place them at the same level. The eye recess can be drilled out with a Forstner bit, if you have one, and/or you can hollow it out with a small gouge. The recess should be slightly bigger than the eye and about ¹⁄₈in (3mm) deep. Put some soft filler into the eye recess and push the glass eye in gently so that the filler squeezes out all round. Smooth off the excess with a palette knife and a damp rag. Before the filler sets hard you may be able to shape it to form an upper eyelid.

PREPARING THE NECK FOR THE MANE

The neck should be prepared for the mane-fixing and it is best to have the mane to hand while you do this, since different types of mane have different fixing methods. A common type

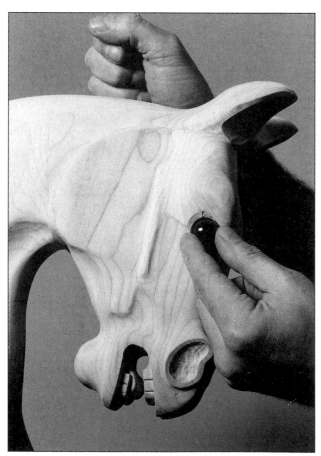

Plate 10.1 Put some soft filler in the eye recess; when the glass eye is pushed in the filler squeezes out all round

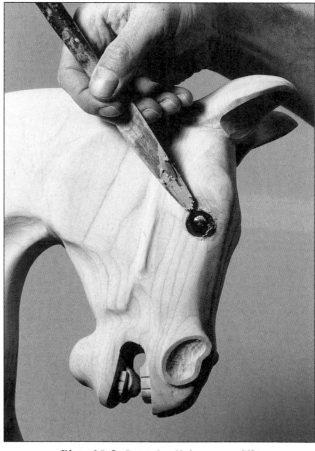

Plate 10.2 Smooth off the excess filler with a palette knife

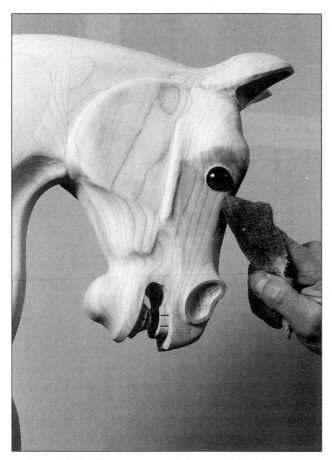

Plate 10.3 Clean up round the eye with a damp rag

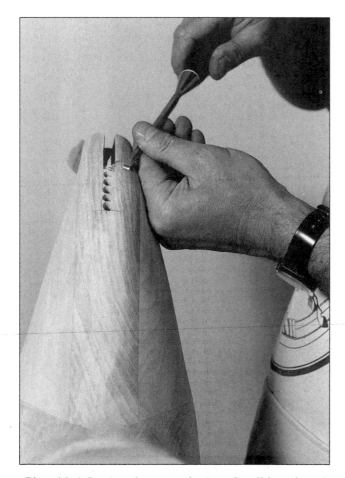

Plate 10.4 Cutting the mane slot in a Small horse's neck

consists of long hair glued and seamed on to a tape which is fitted into a groove or slot cut into the neck of the horse, and secured with wire nails. The groove starts about an inch (25mm) or so behind the base of the ears, and is approximately $3/8$in (10mm) wide and $1/2$in (13mm) deep. It is cut along the horse's neck for the same length as the base of the mane, that is about $7^1/2$in (190mm) for the Small horse, 9in (229mm) for the Medium horse, and $10^1/2$in (267mm) for the Large horse. Mark the position of the slot, drill a row of $1/4$in (6mm) holes, and chisel out. Note that the lower end of the mane stops well short of the front of the saddle so that the hair will not become tangled around the rider's legs.

SADDLE BLOCKS AND STIRRUP STAPLES

Traditional rocking-horse saddles are nailed on, so that there is no chance of the saddle slipping when in use. It is fitted over a wooden saddle block which raises the back of the saddle for a more realistic appearance and a more secure seat for the rider. Refer to the plans in Chapters 6 and 9 to see the size and shape of the saddle

Plate 10.5 Marking the position of the saddle block on the back of a Medium horse

block required for each size of horse. Have the saddle to hand (see next chapter) and place it on the horse's back so that the front runs a little way up the curve of the neck, and pencil mark the back of the saddle. The saddle block is fitted into a groove chiselled out between two sawcuts across the horse's back. The sawcuts are angled back as shown in the plan and the block is set in about $1/2$in (13mm) in the middle. Note that the top of the saddle block is bevelled at about 15°

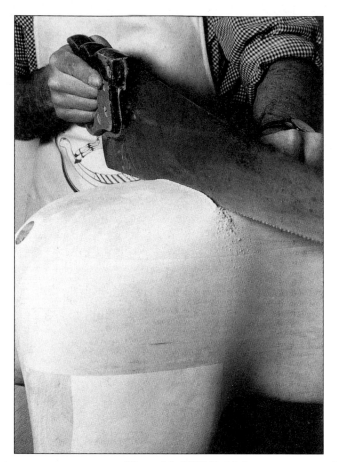

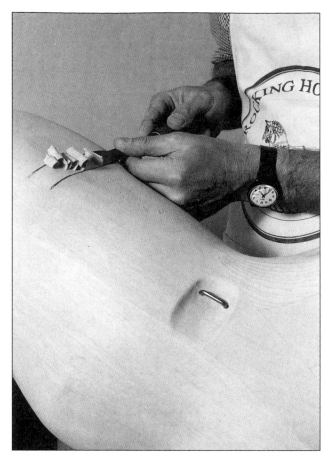

Plates 10.6/10.7 Make two saw cuts for the saddle block and chisel out between

and at either end it is shaped to run smoothly into the horse's back.

The stirrup leathers on Medium and Large horses are usually hung from giant staples hammered securely into the horse. Determine the position of these stirrup staples by placing the saddle on the horse's back, lifting up the skirts, and pencilling round the two oval holes in the flaps (see the next chapter for details of the saddle). With the large gouge hollow out a recess

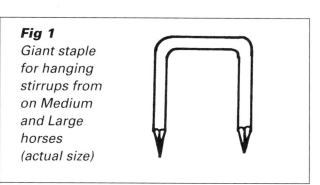

Fig 1
Giant staple for hanging stirrups from on Medium and Large horses (actual size)

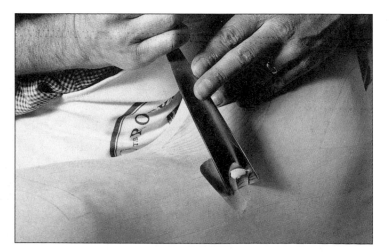

Plate 10.8 On Medium and Large horses gouge out a recess for the stirrup staples

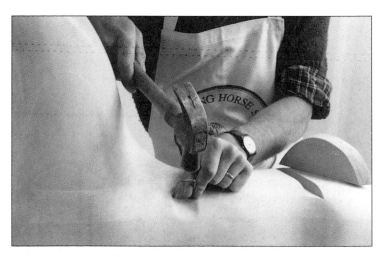

Plate 10.9 Hammer in the giant staples. This picture also shows the saddle block ready to be glued into its slot

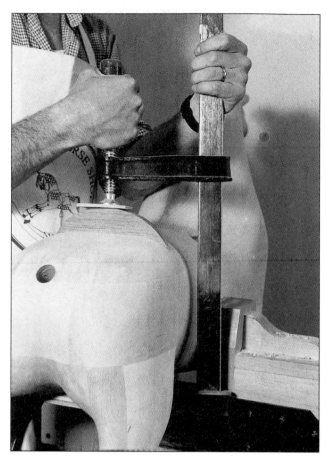

Plate 10.10 Cramping the saddle block in position

*Plate 10.11 Scrim may be glued over the joints with size,
if you are going to apply gesso*

about ³⁄₈in (10mm) deep at each oval. These recesses will allow the stirrup-leather buckle to be run up close to the stirrup staple and lie more or less flat to the side of the horse so that it does not cause an unsightly bulge and, since it is then tucked underneath the skirt, does not rub on the rider's leg. Drill ¹⁄₈in (3mm) pilot holes for the stirrup staples and hammer them in, but do ensure you leave sufficient gap underneath to enable the stirrup leather to be threaded through.

Small horses are not normally fitted with stirrup staples since the stirrup-leather fixing does not require them. Some rocking-horse saddles are made like simplified miniature real ones and simply buckle on with a girth strap. In this case it is not necessary to fit either stirrup staples or a saddle block.

GESSO

The traditional way of preparing the wood prior to painting is to use gesso. This is a mixture of rabbitskin glue and gilder's whiting and is brushed hot on to the bare wood. It acts as a grain filler, covers over rasp marks and other minor blemishes and, after it has dried, can be sanded down to leave a very hard, beautifully smooth surface over which to paint. Also, because the gesso remains slightly flexible even after it has set hard, it will tend to take up slight movements in the underlying timber and minimise cracking of the painted surface, particularly when used in conjunction with scrim over the joints. This flexibility is, however, only very slight; if the underlying timber does move it will probably crack the paintwork anyway, in spite of the gesso. The only way to minimise any tendency to crack is to use properly dried timber and to have good tight joints.

Some makers do not use gesso, regarding it as messy and bothersome. They simply sand the surface smooth and then use a primer and several coats of paint straight on to the wood, rubbing down between each coat to achieve a good finish. But if you decide you would like to do the traditional thing and gesso your horse, the method is as follows.

Soak 3¼oz (92g) of crushed rabbitskin glue overnight in just under two pints (1.1 litres) of cold water, then heat. Do not apply the heat directly but use a glue kettle or a Pyrex bowl over a saucepan of boiling water. Heat the liquid, which is called size, until it begins to steam and you can hardly bear to dip in a finger. Then put it on one side for several hours to cool down to room temperature, when it will set to a khaki-coloured jelly.

Divide the jelly and re-heat half of it. In this way you can add more to the mix as and when you need it, and if you find you will not finish the gessoing in one session, then the remaining jelly can be kept for later use. It will keep quite happily for several days — preferably in a fridge if the weather is warm. Use a 2in (50mm) flat brush and brush the first coat of size only on to the bare wood, all over the horse. Take pieces of scrim (fine-weave-cotton plasterer's scrim) and stick them, with the glue brush, over the joints at the tops of the legs. These are the joints most likely to crack, and I do not normally scrim over any others, but you may wish to do so.

Gently stir in some of the gilder's whiting to give the size body. The consistency of the mix is that of a thin coffee cream which runs easily from the brush. Brush on six or more coats in quick succession, one after the other, and try to alternate the direction of the brushstrokes to give an even build-up. Gesso right over the eyes — after it has dried you can easily scrape it off with a craft knife and clean up the glass eyes with a damp rag. Keep the mixture hot and stir it from time to time as you use it. If the scrim is not being adequately covered you can thicken up the mix with a little more whiting, but it is not necessary to apply the gesso so thickly over the head and lower legs.

As you use the gesso you will lose some of the water through evaporation and it may be necessary to add a drop or two more. If it is too strong, too concentrated, it will set too hard and will crack. Do not add too much water, though, because if it becomes too weak, too dilute, it will be too soft and will clog your abrasive. You can

test the gesso in its jelly form by pressing the surface with two fingers and spreading them so that the jelly cracks apart. The sides of the cracks should have a slightly rough or granular appearance. If they appear smooth the size is too strong and a little water should be added. Over-dilution can be rectified by adding some more glue soaked in very little water.

After gessoing allow the horse to dry out thoroughly for several days before sanding smooth with 150-grit abrasive. It is not unusual to find that a few hairline cracks have appeared as the gesso dries but do not worry about this; just fill them before sanding down. Finally give the horse a coat of thin varnish or primer to seal the surface, and it is ready to proceed with the painting.

PAINTING AND DAPPLING

The painted dapple grey is the characteristic traditional finish for a rocking-horse, and remains the most popular. There are two approaches. For a gloss finish, most ordinary oil-based household paints these days are safe for use on toys as far as lead content is concerned (though they may not comply with all

Plate 10.12 Gesso is brushed liberally all over the horse

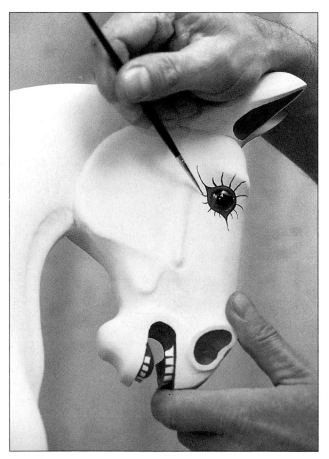

Plate 10.13 You need a steady hand and a fine pencil brush to paint in the eye lashes

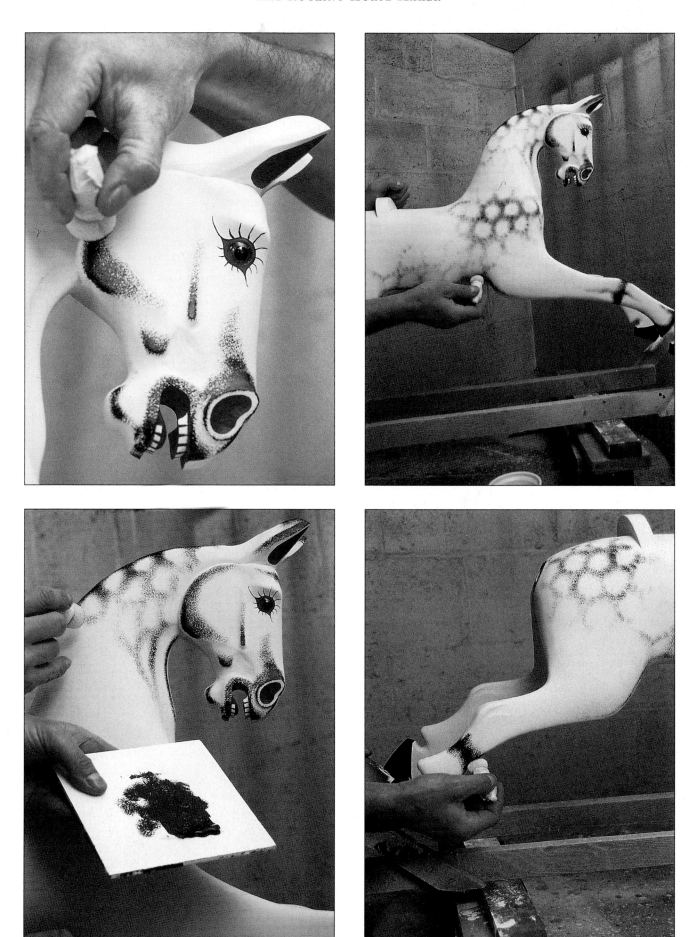

Plates 10.14 – 10.17
Dappling the horse — this is a Small one — using a sponge dappling pad and an old tile for a palette

Plate 10.18 The dappling is complete and the hooves painted black

the latest stringent toy-safety regulations concerning paint finishes — check with your paint supplier if you are worried about this). The base coats should be a pale-grey shade, two or three coats of undercoat, two of gloss, rubbed down gently between each coat, and overlaid with black gloss for dappling and hooves, and deep-red gloss for mouth, nostrils, ears etc. If you use two or more different makes of paint do ensure that they are compatible by testing on a piece of scrap before painting on to the horse, or check with your supplier.

I prefer a less glossy finish, using water-based acrylic paints, which are quick drying and easy to use, and are normally safe on toys (again check with your paint supplier). Start with a one-litre can of white acrylic primer/undercoat and small tubes of acrylic blue (eg ultramarine), deep red (eg cadmium) and black. Take about a quarter of the white undercoat and mix in some blue for the first of the base coats. Put a little of the primer to one side for touching up the teeth later, and then thoroughly mix some of the black with the rest to make a pale shade of grey for the remainder of the base coats. Three coats will be enough; rub down lightly between each coat and stir in a little water if the

consistency seems too thick — try to ensure that the final base coat leaves the surface smooth.

When applying base coats you can paint right over the glass eyes. Then, when the paint has dried, run the point of a craft knife round the eyes and peel off the paint, which does not stick too well to glass. Use the red paint to rim the eyes, and to paint in the inside of the ears, nostrils and mouth. You will need a thin pencil brush for this, and to delineate the teeth. Carefully paint in the eyelashes with black; black is also used for the hooves, and for the dappling.

Traditional-style dappling is applied freehand with a dappling pad made from a piece of sponge rubber around which may be wrapped a piece of stockinette which leaves an interesting 'hairy' appearance. Squeeze some black paint on to a scrap of wood or an old tile and dip the dappling pad into it, then dab it on to the horse. Start near the top of the neck and keep dabbing until the dabs form a circle with an area of the base coat showing in the middle, then move on to dab another circle, and so on. It is important to use a dabbing action — do not smear the paint or you will make a mess of it. The first dabs will leave a lot of black, but as the

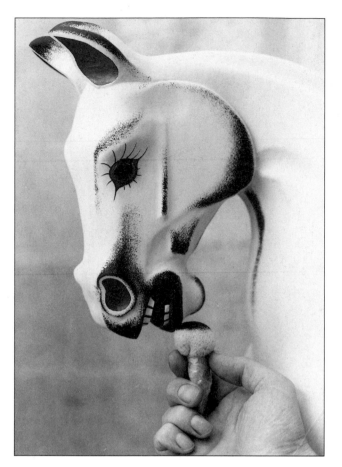

Plate 10.19 The dappling of Medium (shown here) or Large horses is done in the same way as for the Small

Plate 10.20 A Medium horse with dappling complete. Note the dappling on the neck

paint is used up the dabs become lighter and you can vary the intensity of the dappling to achieve an interesting surface. The dappling should be roughly symmetrical on both sides of the horse.

It is possible to pre-determine the positions of the dapples by sticking circles cut from thin card on to the horse with double-sided masking tape or Blutack. The dappling can also be applied with a short-bristle stencil brush (keep it almost dry), or air brush or spray. It is advisable to test out your dappling technique on a piece of scrap wood before attempting the horse.

Rocking-horses painted with acrylics should be varnished all over with a clear matt or satin varnish. The varnish softens the appearance of the dappling and protects the surface from finger marking. It is not necessary to varnish over oil-based gloss paints, though you may wish to do so.

ANTIQUE PAINT

For a more authentic-looking 'antique' finish you can apply an antique glaze to horses painted in acrylics, after the dappling has dried but before the final varnish. The antique glaze is a

mixture of varnish, linseed oil and turpentine (approx proportions, $4:1:\frac{1}{2}$) and a dash of Vandyke brown. It is brushed liberally all over the horse and then, before it has dried, ragged off with a clean cotton cloth. The glaze leaves the horse nicely discoloured and interesting variations in colour can be achieved by wiping more glaze off the high spots. The glaze may take several days to thoroughly dry out before you can apply the final coat of varnish.

ALTERNATIVE FINISHES

You may prefer a paint finish other than the traditional dapple grey, for example piebald, palomino, black or white. It is usual to give them socks and a blaze in a contrasting colour. Do bear in mind, though, that an all-over plain colour will show up every imperfection in the surface. (This is a major advantage of the dapple grey — the fact that dappling breaks up the surface and helps to mask imperfections probably accounts for the popularity of this method among traditional rocking-horse makers.)

However, you may opt for a natural-wood finish. Why cover the natural beauty of the wood? In our experience traditionally painted rocking-horses are preferred by children while natural

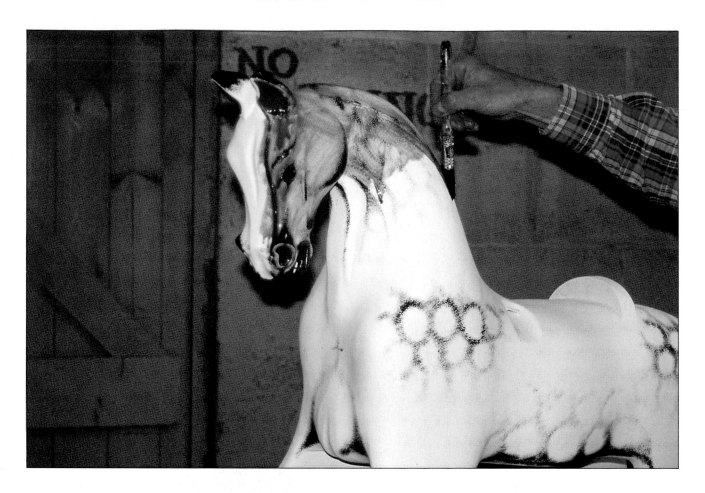

Plate 10.21 This medium horse is being painted with an antique glaze. It looks as if it is making a real mess of the paintwork

wood has a more adult appeal. Since many rocking-horses are regarded as prized artefacts and pieces of furniture, rather than as just children's playthings, a natural-wood finish can be an attractive proposition, either stained and lacquered or varnished and polished. You will have to prepare the surface of the wood by very thorough sanding with progressively finer grit papers. You will also want to make sure that your joints are all as good as can be, since all 'mistakes' or blemishes will be seen.

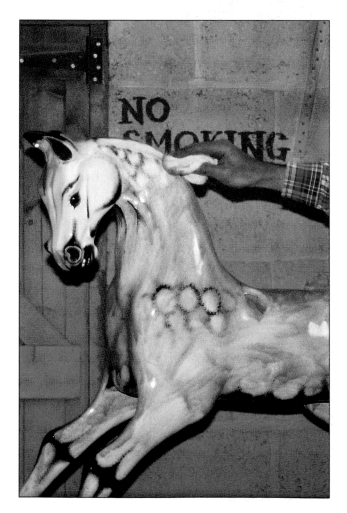

Plate 10.22 Wiping off surplus glaze with a cotton rag

100

Plate 10.23 After ragging off, the paint surface is left pleasantly discoloured and 'mellow'

CHAPTER 11

LEATHER TACK AND HAIR
FOR CARVED HORSES

SADDLES

Rocking-horses can be fitted with many different types and styles of saddle, from the very simple and basic to saddles that buckle on with a girth, made like miniature real ones. I tend to favour nailed-on saddles which cannot slip when in use, and Figs 2 and 3 show the parts of a typical traditional-style saddle and saddlecloths suitable for use on the carved horses in this book. The main dimensions for each of the three sizes of horse are given in the table below.

The saddle should be made from a good-quality vegetable-tanned leather and the top is stuffed with cotton or foam-rubber padding.

	Small Horse	Medium Horse	Large Horse
Dimension A	13in (330mm)	16in (406mm)	18in (457mm)
Dimension B	4¼in (108mm)	5¼in (133mm)	6¼in (159mm)
Dimension C	6½in (165mm)	7¾in (197mm)	9in (229mm)
Dimension D	7in (178mm)	9½in (241mm)	11in (279mm)
Cantle Strap	8in (203mm)	9½in (241mm)	11in (279mm)
Dimension E	7in (178mm)	10½in (267mm)	13in (330mm)
Dimension F	6in (152mm)	6½in (165mm)	8in (203mm)

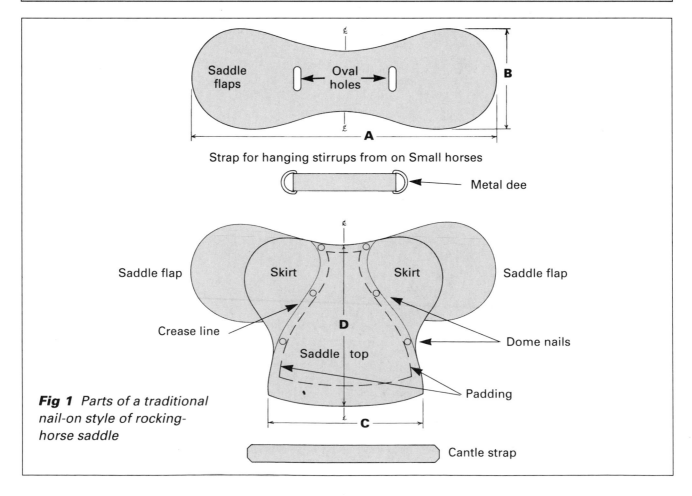

Strap for hanging stirrups from on Small horses

Metal dee

Saddle flap — Skirt — Skirt — Saddle flap

Crease line

Dome nails

Saddle top

Padding

Cantle strap

Fig 1 *Parts of a traditional nail-on style of rocking-horse saddle*

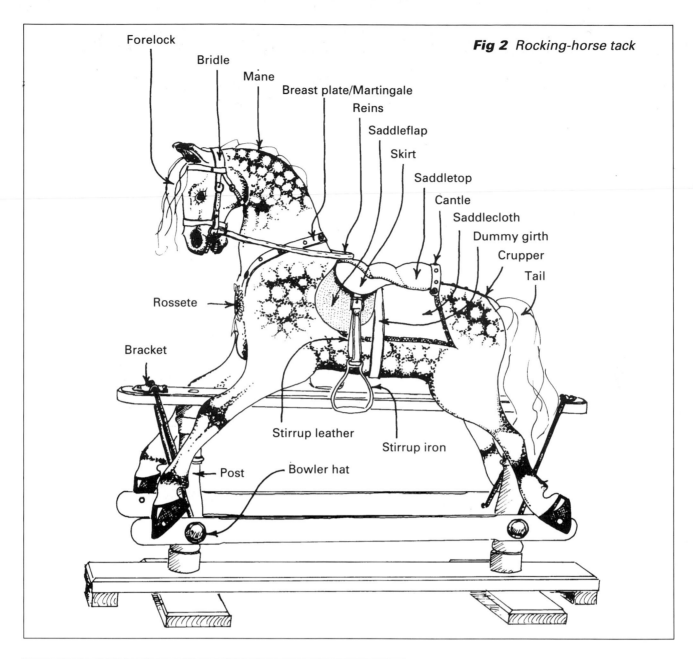

Fig 2 Rocking-horse tack

Forelock
Bridle
Mane
Breast plate/Martingale
Reins
Saddleflap
Skirt
Saddletop
Cantle
Saddlecloth
Dummy girth
Crupper
Tail
Rossete
Bracket
Stirrup leather
Stirrup iron
Post
Bowler hat

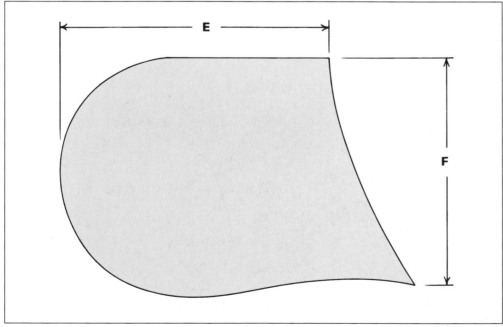

Fig 3
Shape of saddlecloth,
usually edged with
fancy braid

E

F

The saddlecloths can be made from thin leather or coloured leathercloth with a fancy woven braid stitched round the edges, and these are fitted first. The back of the saddlecloth lines up with the back of the saddle block and the top edges will be concealed under the saddle top. They are fixed in place (as is all the leatherwork except the bridle) with 1in (25mm)-round wire nails. Make sure that you pull the saddlecloths

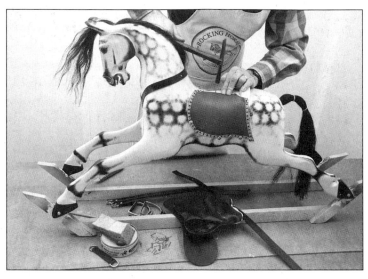

Plate 11.1 Nailing on the saddlecloths. Stretch them as tight as you can over the contours of the horse

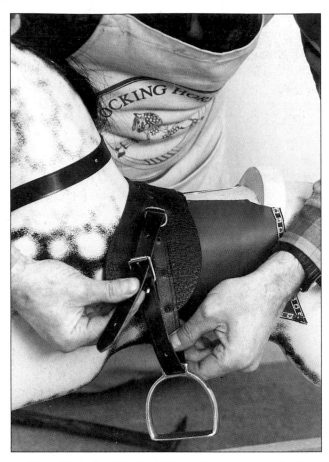

Plate 11.3 On this Small horse the stirrup leather is being threaded through the dees at either side

Plate 11.2 A dummy girth has been nailed over the saddlecloths and the saddle flaps are then nailed on

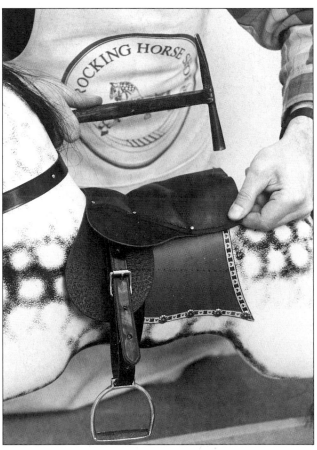

Plate 11.4 Hold the saddle top down firmly as you nail it on, starting from the front

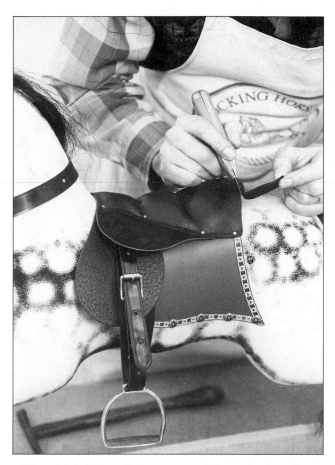

Plate 11.5 *Trim off the excess saddle-top leather along the saddle block*

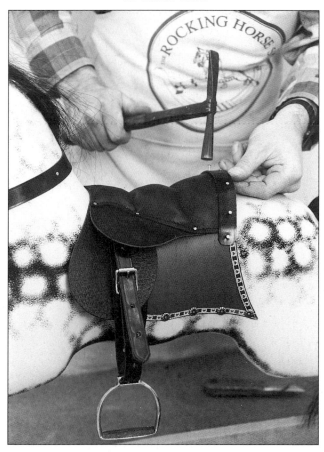

Plate 11.6 *The cantle strap hides any roughness at the back of the saddle*

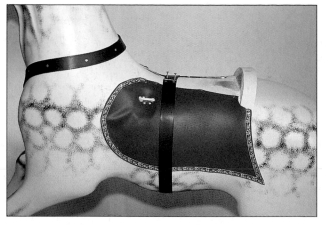

Plate 11.7 *On Medium (or Large) horses the saddle-cloth is cut to reveal the staples from which the stirrup leathers will hang. Note the dummy girth, nailed in place at the top*

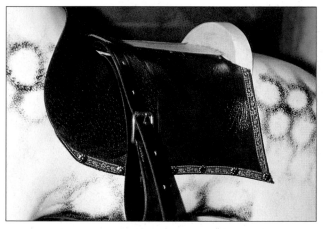

Plate 11.8 *The saddlecloths on this Medium horse are a more subdued 'antique' leather. The stirrup leathers are threaded through oval holes in the saddle flaps and round the stirrup staple*

as tight as you can over the contours of the horse before hammering home the wire nails. The heads of these wire nails are later concealed beneath the heads of fancy-head nails hammered in close alongside them.

Next fit a dummy girth by taking a length of $\frac{7}{8}$in (22mm)-wide strapping right round the horse's body at the fattest part. Pull it tight and nail in place at the top middle. A nail underneath the belly at either side will hold the dummy girth firmly in place.

On Medium and Large horses the saddle-cloths will have covered the stirrup staples, concealing them, so with a sharp knife or scissors cut the saddlecloth material along the line of the stirrup staples, and nail the cut edges in behind the staples. The saddle flaps are fixed in place with a couple of nails in the middle so that the oval holes align with the stirrup staples. If you damp the leather before fitting you will be able to stretch it so that it conforms to the

Plate 11.9 Detail of threading stirrup leather for Medium (or Large) horse

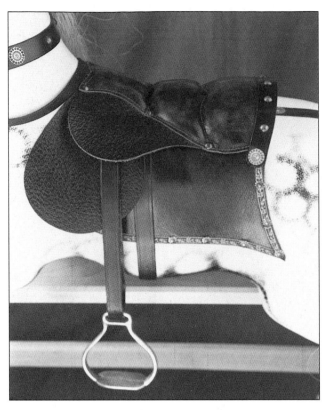

Plate 11.11 Complete saddle on a Medium horse. Note the dome and fancy nails

Plate 11.10 Nailing on the saddle top

contours of the horse. Stirrup leathers are made from ¾in (19mm) strap with a buckle at one end: 21in, 24in and 28in (533mm, 610mm and 710mm) long for Small, Medium and Large horses respectively. Thread them in through the oval hole in the saddle flaps, under the stirrup staple, and back out through the oval hole, then do up the buckle. For suppliers of ready-made saddles, stirrup irons and other rocking-horse accessories, see Appendix 2.

On Small horses (or old horses that do not have stirrup staples), two brass dees are attached to a length of ¾in (19mm) strap as shown in Fig 2. This is then nailed on to the horse's back in the middle so that the dees stick out through the oval holes in the saddle flaps

and both of the stirrup leathers can be threaded through.

Place the saddle top in position. Again you can damp the leather to make it more amenable, and with the front edge aligned with the front of the saddle flap and in the middle, tap in a nail at the stitched corner at each side. Press down firmly on the saddle top and carry on nailing it down along each side. Fixing nails should be evenly spaced at each side. Adjust the padding, or remove some, so that the top fits back neatly against and over the saddle block. Any of the saddle top leather which overhangs the saddle block at the back should be trimmed off with a sharp knife or scissors. The cantle is a length of ¾in (19mm)-wide leather nailed over the saddle block to hide any roughness and give a neat finish to the back of the saddle.

As mentioned earlier, sometimes saddles are used which buckle on with a girth strap. They have a loose saddleblanket which is laid over the horse's back and the saddle is placed on it. Buckle the girth strap tight. You should drive two small screws through holes in the girth under the belly, leaving the heads proud. These screws help to prevent the girth from slipping round when in use, and if the heads of the screws used are small enough, will still allow the saddle to be lifted off. Although it is an attrac-

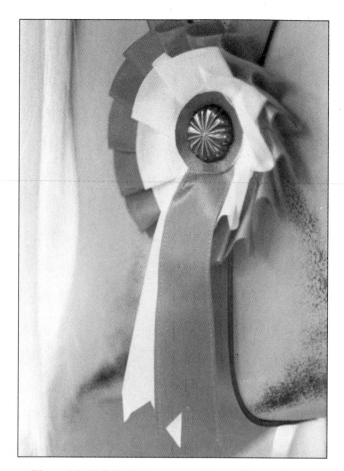

Plates 11.12/11.13 A rosette, either ribbon or leather, is fixed with a large fancy nail in the centre of the chest where the chest straps converge

tive idea to have a removable saddle we cannot recommend them very strongly since they can never be as secure as the nail-on type. The stirrup leathers on girth-type saddles hang from dees located under the skirts.

A superior version of the girth-strap-type saddle is sometimes fitted on very-high-class rocking-horses. These saddles are handmade round a wooden tree, just like a miniature real one. Two wooden pegs in the underside of the saddle are made to locate into two holes in the horse's back. The saddle therefore will not slip at all if the girth is kept buckled tight, but the saddle can still be removed.

MARTINGALE AND CRUPPER

To form the simplified and decorative breast plate or martingale, a length of leather strapping is taken round the horse's neck and cut off so that the ends meet neatly at a point in the centre of the chest. From this point a further length of strap is taken downwards and nailed in under the horse. Decorative dome and/or fancy nails are spaced evenly along the strap. A ribbon rosette is nailed on at the centre of the chest over the point where the chest straps converge.

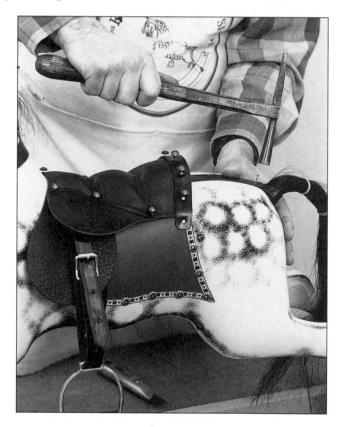

Plate 11.14 Nailing on the tail strap (crupper). Note the dome-headed nails which will be driven in close alongside the wire nails

After the tail is secured (see below), take a short length of strap, wrap it round the base of the tail and nail together at the top. Another length of strap is nailed on so that it runs from the centre of the saddle block back to the top of the base of the tail. This crupper helps to give the tail a bit of lift, and hides any roughness there may be at the base of the tail.

As mentioned above, dome or decorative nails are driven in close beside the wire nails you have used to fix the saddle and saddle-cloths, and along the breast plate and crupper, where they will help to keep the leatherwork securely in place and enhance the appearance.

BRIDLES

Traditionally, rocking-horses had leather strapping nailed on to the head to form a bridle, and of course you can fit this type if you wish. But we prefer to use bridles that have a bit and reins attached and simply buckle on. It is a nice thing for children to be able to remove the bridle in their play, and you do not have to hammer nails into the horse's head. Fig 4 shows a very simple buckle-on bridle which can be made from $\frac{1}{2}$in (13mm)-wide leather strap. Fig 5 shows an 'improved' type, more like a real one. Leather tack can be kept supple and clean by occasional applications of saddle soap or leather oil.

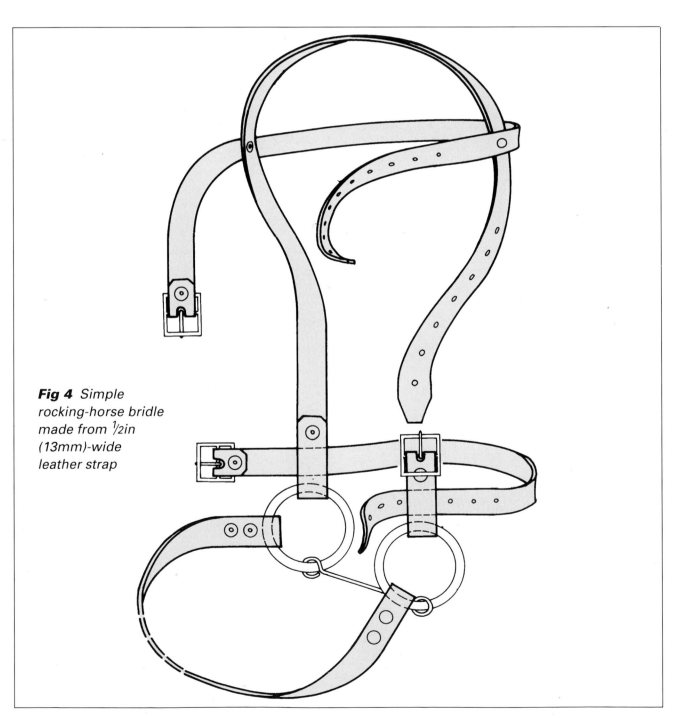

Fig 4 Simple rocking-horse bridle made from $\frac{1}{2}$in (13mm)-wide leather strap

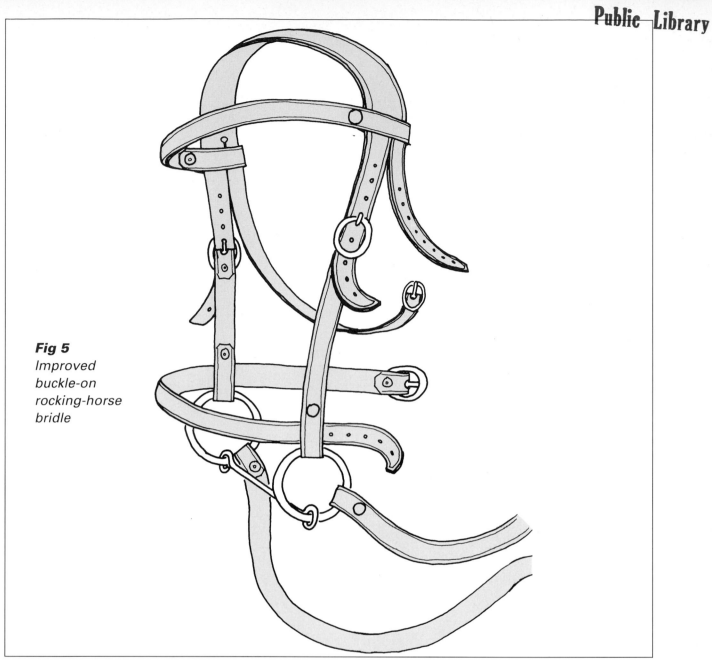

Fig 5
Improved buckle-on rocking-horse bridle

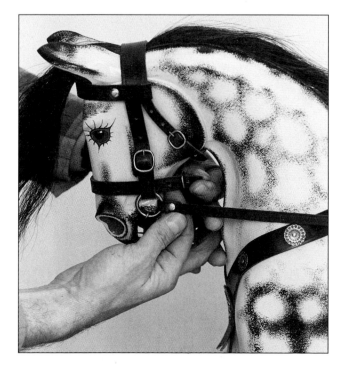

MANES AND TAILS

Hair may be either simulated or real horsehair. Push the seam of the mane into the slot cut in the horse's neck, using a blunt screwdriver or coin and nail in place with a thin leather strip. Pull the hair to the left and nail in a second thin leather strip. It is obviously important to fix the mane securely since children will tug at it (see Fig 6). The mane hair finishes up under the first leather strip and up one side of the second strip, all firmly secured in place with 1in (25mm)-round wire nails. The hair is then allowed to fall to the right so that it conceals the fixing. A small bunch of hair is taken forward between the ears to form the forelock. There is a tendency for the hair to stick up at odd angles; simulated hair can be persuaded to lie down by

Plate 11.15 Buckling the bridle on to a Small horse

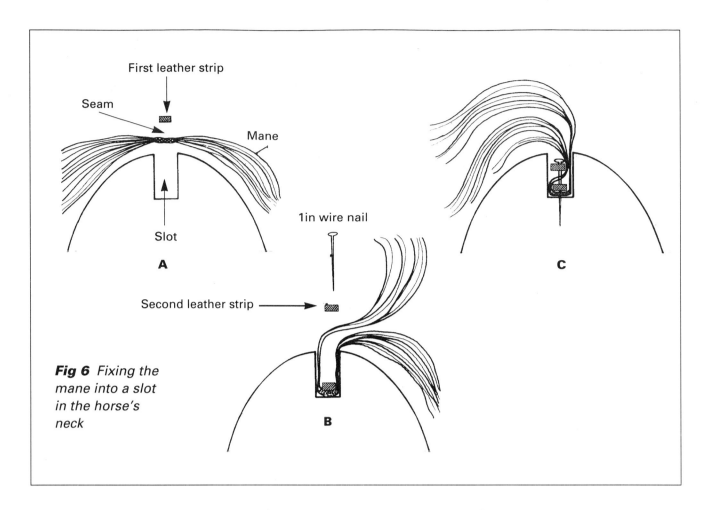

First leather strip

Seam

Mane

Slot

A

1in wire nail

Second leather strip

B

C

Fig 6 *Fixing the mane into a slot in the horse's neck*

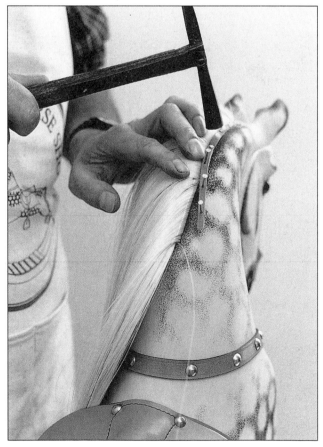

Plate 11.16 Wedging a seamed mane into its slot with the first leather strip

Plate 11.17 With the hair pulled left, the second leather strip is nailed into the slot to fix the mane securely

Plate 11.18 A small bunch of hair is brought forward between the ears to form the forelock. The head strap of the bridle will help to hold this in place. This Small horse has a simulated hair mane

Plate 11.20 Detail of base of tail

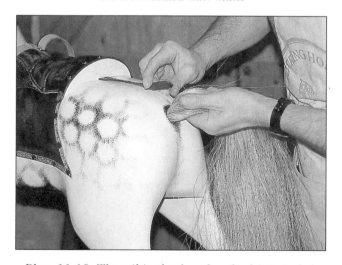

Plate 11.19 The tail is glued and wedged into its hole

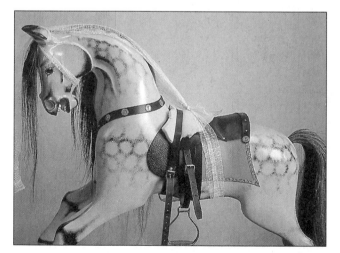

Plate 11.21 If the hair sticks up at odd angles damp it and tie it down

blowing warm air over it (not too hot!) with a hair drier. Horsehair is persuaded to lie down by damping it or rubbing in ordinary hair conditioner and tying it down in position with some strips of cloth or a bandage and leaving overnight.

There are other types of mane with different methods of fixing them. Some are secured into a slot with glue or resin. Real horsehair manes on the hide are particularly suitable for restoring old rocking-horses, and do not require a slot in the neck.

Fit the tail by squeezing some glue into the hole, push in the tail and secure by tapping in a small wooden wedge underneath. Finally, the hair can be combed out, trimmed and layered as desired. There will be some hair loss at first but this should soon settle down. Simulated hair in particular has a tendency to get tangled and matted so should be combed out regularly. Once the horse has been all tacked up to your satisfaction, remove it from the temporary hoof rails and lift it on to the stand. Drill the hoof-bolt holes right through the hoof rails, tighten up the nuts, and, at last, he's ready to ride!

Plate 11.22 Small horse on bows, with natural wood finish, all tacked up and ready to ride

Plate 11.23 Child's eye view of the Large horse

Plate 11.24 A Large horse being given its first test ride!

CHAPTER 12
A MINIATURE ROCKING-HORSE FOR A DOLLS' HOUSE

This is a twelfth-scale dolls'-house-size version of the Large rocking-horse described in Chapter 9. I found that making a rocking-horse on such a small scale after being accustomed to the full-size versions presented peculiar problems; you certainly need a good eye and steady hand and everything has to be handled so much more delicately. On the other hand few tools are needed, the materials are relatively inexpensive, and the whole project, including tools, can be kept in a small shoe box.

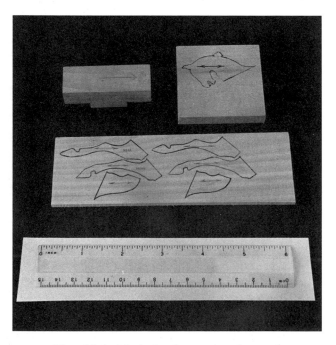

Plate 12.1 Mark the shape on to the wood, and note the direction of grain

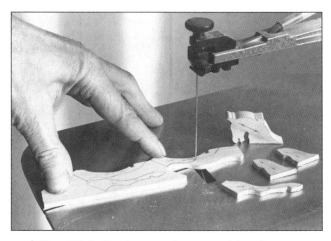

Plate 12.2 Cutting out the parts with a fret saw

TIMBER

The horse is made from lime, basswood or similar timber. Model craft suppliers often stock prepared timber in suitable thicknesses, but avoid balsa, which is really too fragile.

Cutting list

	Thickness x width x length			Thickness x width x length		
	Inches			**Millimetres**		
Head and neck	$^{25}/_{64}$ x $1^{1}/_{2}$ x $2^{3}/_{8}$			10 x 38 x 60		
Body	$^{25}/_{32}$ x $^{25}/_{32}$ x $2^{3}/_{8}$			20 x 20 x 60		
All 4 legs and 2 neck-muscle blocks	$^{5}/_{32}$ x 2 x $5^{1}/_{2}$			4 x 50 x 140		
Saddle block	$^{1}/_{8}$ x $^{1}/_{4}$ x $^{5}/_{8}$			3 x 6 x 16		

Plate 12.3 Mark the body for the leg notches

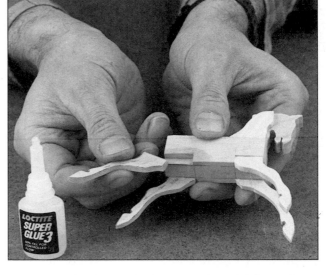

Plate 12.4 Glueing the horse together with Superglue

PATTERNS

Trace the patterns for the head and neck, legs and neck-muscle blocks on to the wood and cut out carefully with a fret saw. Avoid having short grain running across those parts vulnerable to breakage (ie legs and ears) by keeping the direction of grain running in approximately the same direction as the arrows on the plan.

PREPARING THE BODY

The body is a solid block and should be marked for the notch at each corner to receive the legs. These notches can be cut out with a sharp chisel or knife and note that they are angled so that the legs splay out, leaving $9/16$in (14mm) between the legs at the body end, and $13/16$in (20mm) between the hooves (approximately!). Mark the body block with an arrow pointing to the front, and glue on the neck, making sure that it is central. Then glue on the neck-muscle blocks at either side. Use aliphatic resin glue and small cramps, or Superglue, in which case you need no cramps, for the assembly. Then glue on the legs. It is a good idea to give extra security to the leg fixings by dowelling them to the body. Wooden cocktail sticks make good dowels. Drill two holes to fit your cocktail sticks through the top of each leg and into the body. Put a little glue on to the dowel, push in firmly and cut off neatly.

CARVING

When the glue has set the carving can commence. You will need a really sharp small pointed knife for this, a scalpel is ideal, and of course you will have to take care not to cut yourself (too many times). Remove all the square

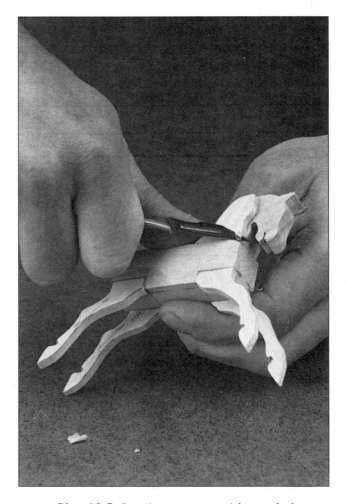

Plate 12.5 Starting to carve, with a scalpel

corners, taking a little from each side in turn to keep the symmetry, and carving gradually towards the rocking-horse shape. You will probably find it helpful to refer to the photographs in Chapters 6 and 9. Of course, each person's carving is unique – this is what gives each horse its own character.

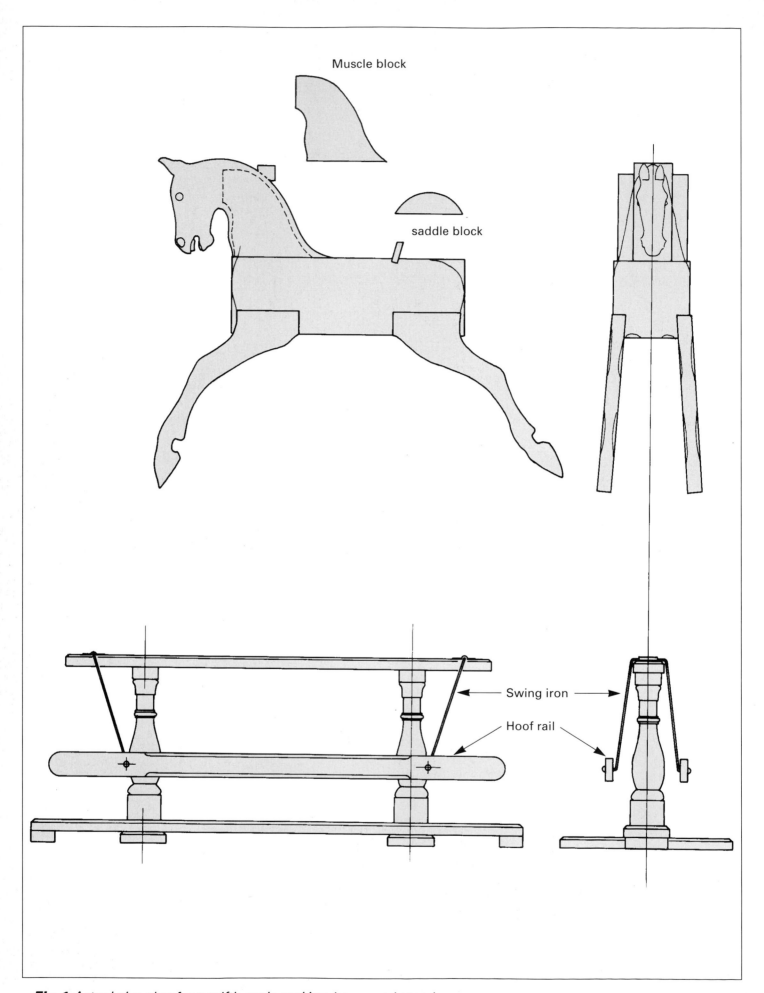

Muscle block

saddle block

Swing iron

Hoof rail

Fig 1 *Actual-size plan for twelfth-scale rocking-horse and stand*

Plate 12.6 Twelfth-scale rocking-horse for a dolls' house

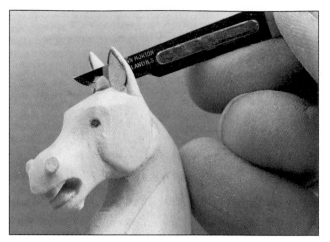

Plate 12.7 Carefully carving ears

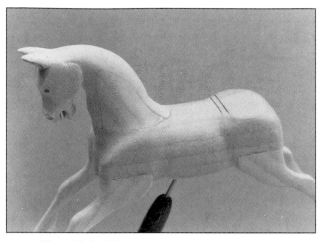

*Plate 12.8 The carving virtually complete —
note the marks for the saddle block*

When you start to carve the head, mark the cheeks and the eye positions. The head tapers to approximately $^3/_{16}$in (5mm) wide at the mouth. Carve the teeth with care since the grain is short here and it is all too easy to end up with a toothless horse. If you have one, a small round burr tool will be useful for hollowing out the nostrils and ears.

*Plate 12.9 Drilling the tail hole.
The saddle block has been fitted*

FINISHING OFF

When you are happy with the shape of your horse, sand him all over with 180-grit abrasive paper to remove your carving marks, then with finer-grade abrasive papers — 240 and even 360 grit to achieve a nicely rounded smooth finish. Take particular care when sanding the head, ears and hooves, to leave your carving sharp. Mark the position for the saddle block, cut a $^1/_8$in (3mm)-wide groove, glue the saddle block in place and then sand lightly so that the edges run smoothly into the horse. Drill a $^3/_{32}$in (2mm) hole for the tail.

Rub a grain filler all over the horse with your finger tips, and sand smooth with very fine abrasive paper. Give the horse a coat of sanding sealer and when dry, lightly sand again. Use acrylics for the painting; give the horse two or three coats of pale grey, lightly sanding between coats. Paint on the black dapples with the end of a cocktail stick or a very fine pencil brush — have a practice first — and paint the hooves black. Two tiny pins are used for the eyes, which

Plate 12.10 Sealed, sanded and painted pale grey

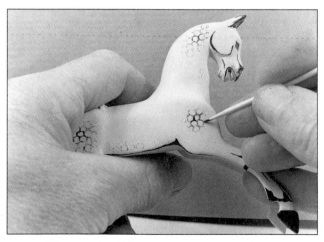

Plate 12.11 Dappling with a cocktail stick

Plate 12.12 Bridle and reins

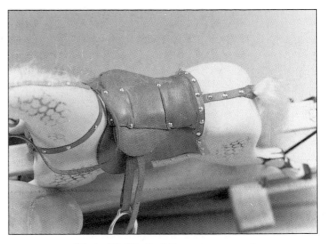

Plate 12.13 Saddle arrangement

are painted brown with a black dot for the iris, and rimmed with red. Also the mouth, the inside of the ears and the nostrils are painted red. Finally, the horse is given a thin coat of matt or satin acrylic varnish.

FITTING THE TACK

The leather for the saddlery will have to be skived, that is thinned down by shaving off the suede side with a sharp knife until it is very thin. Cut strips approximately $\frac{1}{32}$in (1mm) wide for the bridle, $\frac{1}{16}$in (2mm) wide for the martingale, stirrup leathers and crupper. Glue the martingale on to the horse (with white PVA glue) secured with tiny nails. The tiny nails are pushed in, and it may make this easier if you drill tiny guide holes. Put the saddlery on to the horse starting with the saddlecloths, which are cut from red carpet tape, and edged with $\frac{1}{16}$in (2mm)-wide ribbon, glued on and decorated with the tiny nails evenly spaced. The chest rosette is made from $\frac{1}{16}$in (2mm) ribbon and fixed with a slightly larger nail. The leather saddle seat is cut and folded and glued on, and edged with tiny nails. Most of the accessories suitable for this horse, including tiny stirrups, brackets, leather and tiny nails, etc, are available from suppliers of miniature accessories; see Appendix 2.

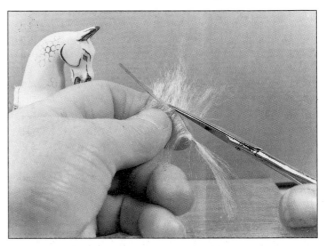

Plate 12.14 Preparing the mane

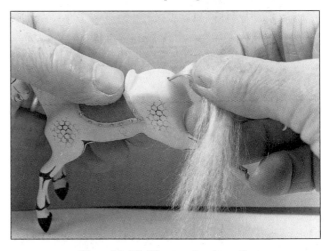

Plate 12.15 Glueing in the tail – note saddlecloth has been fitted

THE MANE AND TAIL

The mane and tail are made from embroidery thread carefully teased out with a stiff toothbrush to separate the fibres. For the mane, glue the fibres on to a $\frac{1}{32}$in (1mm)-wide strip of leather, cut off flush at one side and glue on to the neck, leaving a piece of hair to hang between the ears to form the forelock. For the tail, glue together the ends of the fibres, roll up and glue into the hole, and push in a small

wooden wedge to hold the tail up at a jaunty angle. Finally fit the crupper and bridle. The bridle 'cheek pieces' are led to two tiny brass bit rings to which the reins are also attached.

THE STAND

Now for the stand. Prepare the wood as in the cutting list overleaf, which gives the required finished sizes.

Cutting list: *The Miniature Stand*

	Thickness x width x length						Thickness x width x length				
	Inches						**Millimetres**				
Top rail	$^1\!/_8$	x	$^5\!/_{16}$	x	$4^3\!/_8$		3	x	8	x	110
Bottom rail	$^1\!/_8$	x	$^{15}\!/_{32}$	x	5		3	x	12	x	127
Cross-pieces (x 2)	$^1\!/_8$	x	$^{15}\!/_{32}$	x	$1^3\!/_4$		3	x	12	x	45
End-pieces (x 2)	$^1\!/_8$	x	$^1\!/_4$	x	$^7\!/_{16}$		3	x	6	x	11
Posts (x 2)	$^{13}\!/_{32}$	x	$^{13}\!/_{32}$	x	$1^7\!/_8$		10	x	10	x	48
Hoof rails (x 2)	$^1\!/_{16}$	x	$^1\!/_4$	x	$4^5\!/_8$		2	x	6	x	118

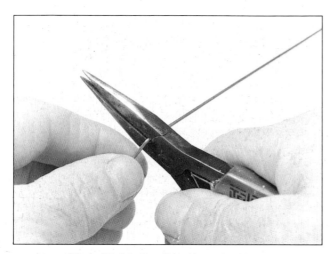

Plate 12.16 Bending the swing irons

Chamfer the top edges of the stand rails and cross-pieces. The posts can be left square, or tapered, or if you have a suitable lathe, turned to the pattern shown. If turned, leave a $^1\!/_8$in (3mm)-diameter peg $^5\!/_{32}$in (4mm) long top and bottom, and reduce the diameter of the post at the top to $^9\!/_{32}$in (7mm). The posts are $1^5\!/_8$in (40mm) long between the top and bottom rails.

Mark the positions of the posts carefully on the top rail. Hold the top rail centrally on the bottom rail and carefully drill a $^1\!/_8$in (3mm) hole through both pieces. Also drill a $^1\!/_8$in (3mm)-diameter hole $^1\!/_{32}$in (1mm) into the exact centre of the cross-piece, then glue it all together. If you have left the posts square (or tapered them), you can cut them off to the exact length between the rails, which is $1^5\!/_8$in (40mm), and fix them in place with cocktail-stick dowel pegs. Glue on the end-pieces and, when dry, trim off the pegs or dowels at the tops and bottoms of the posts and lightly sand smooth. Make the hoof rails and drill $^5\!/_{64}$in (2mm) holes for the swing irons. Lightly sand, stain and varnish the stand and hoof rails.

Make the swing irons by bending $^1\!/_{32}$in (1mm) brass wire to the shape of the pattern. Ensure both are the same. Tiny brackets are available to secure swing irons to the top rail of the stand and are fixed on with tiny nails. Cut notches in the hooves so they will fit over the hoof rails and glue them on. Drill through hooves and hoof rails and push through a tiny nail to hold it securely. Fit the ends of the swing irons through the holes in the hoof rails. The ends can be secured with a nut which is glued on. Make sure that the swing irons move freely and that the horse rocks properly; then stand back and wait for admiring looks.

Plate 12.17 Miniature rocking-horse in dolls' house nursery

Plate 12.18 The completed Miniature rocking-horse

CHAPTER 13
A CAROUSEL-STYLE HORSE

T his design is based on a style of horse common on small English merry-go-rounds in the early part of this century. The construction has been kept as straightforward as possible, the head and legs being straight, not turned or splayed, in order to make the carving of the detail, on which the success of the project depends, relatively unproblematic. Nevertheless, this is a more ambitious wood-carving project than a rocking-horse, and it presents an interesting challenge.

Unlike rocking-horses, the carousel or merry-go-round style of horse traditionally has the bridle and saddlery, mane and forelock all carved on the horse. Sometimes the tail as well would be carved wood, but more usually it was horse hair. The construction is broadly similar to making a small rocking-horse, consisting of blocks of timber bandsawn to shape and glued and pegged together, due allowance being made for the carving of the extra superficial details of saddlery and mane. The head and legs are cut from thicker timber than for a rocking-horse, giving greater scope for shaping these parts, and rendering eye and ear pieces and leg-muscle blocks unnecessary.

Before starting refer back to Chapter 2, since much of the information on tools and timber etc, applies to this project. Choose a good carving timber such as tulipwood or lime and prepare your timber according to the cutting list below, which gives the finished sizes required.

MARKING THE PATTERNS
Mark out the patterns on the timber for the head and neck, neck-muscle blocks, and legs, making sure that the direction of grain conforms approximately with the arrows on Fig 1. Note where cramping flats or noggins are to be left on the timber before bandsawing out the shapes, and that the legs have tenons attached to them. These are bare-faced tenons and are to be set into mortices chopped in the under side of the lower-body block. They are $3/4$in (19mm) thick and $1\frac{1}{4}$in (32mm) deep, 3in (76mm) long for the front legs, $3\frac{1}{2}$in (89mm) long for the rear legs, in the positions shown on the plan.

Cutting list

| | Thickness x width x length | | | | Thickness x width x length | | |
	Inches				Millimetres		
Head and neck	$2^3/4$	x 8	x 14	70	x 203	x 356
Neck-muscle blocks (1st and 2nd)	$3/4$	x $7^3/4$	x 18	19	x 197	x 457
Upper-body block	$1^3/4$	x $5^3/4$	x $19^3/4$	45	x 146	x 502
Lower-body block	$1^3/4$	x $5^3/4$	x 20	45	x 146	x 508
Mid-body blocks (sides) (x 2)	$1^3/4$	x $3^1/4$	x 20	45	x 83	x 508
Mid-body blocks (ends) (x 2)	$1^3/4$	x $3^1/4$	x $2^3/8$	45	x 83	x 60
Back of saddle	$1^3/4$	x $4^1/4$	x 5	45	x 108	x 127
Legs (all four)	$1^3/8$	x $7^3/4$	x 44	35	x 197	x 1,118

Before you start on the assembly drill a ³⁄₄in (19mm) hole for the supporting pole through both upper- and lower-body blocks. This hole is 7in (178mm) from the front of the lower-body block, but note that the upper-body block is set back by ³⁄₁₆in (5mm) so the hole is 6¹³⁄₁₆in (173mm) from the front of the upper-body block. After the neck has been fixed on you will need to extend this pole hole up through the cramping noggin.

Plate 13.1 Fitting leg tenon into mortice in the under-side of the lower-body block

ASSEMBLY

As with rocking-horse making you can do some of the rough carving and shaping of the head and legs prior to assembly, or if you prefer you can do all the assembly and then start to carve. Make sure your leg tenons are a good tight fit into their mortices and glue and cramp them in. Then glue on the middle-body blocks, using three fluted-dowel pegs along each side. The neck is glued down centrally on to the upper-body block using two or three fluted-dowel pegs and the first and then second neck-muscle blocks are glued on at either side.

You will see that the first neck-muscle block for the left side is bigger than the other one because the mane will be carved on the left side of the neck. The reason for this is merely an acknowledgement of the tradition: English merry-go-rounds go clockwise and therefore the

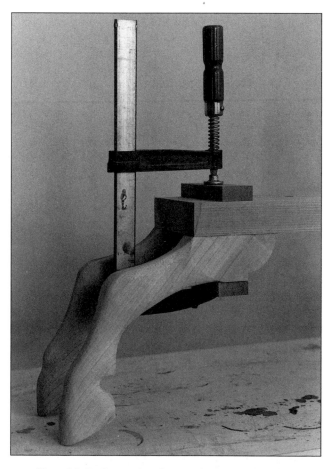

Plate 13.2 Cramping legs to the lower-body block

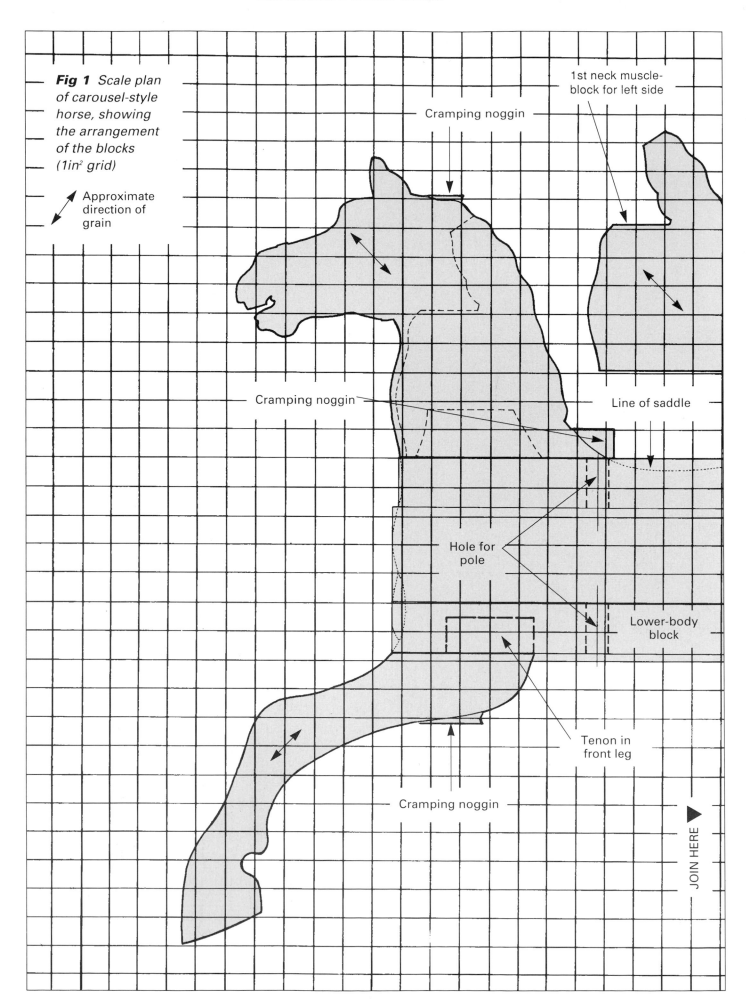

Fig 1 *Scale plan of carousel-style horse, showing the arrangement of the blocks (1in² grid)*

Approximate direction of grain

Cramping noggin

1st neck muscle-block for left side

Cramping noggin

Line of saddle

Hole for pole

Lower-body block

Tenon in front leg

Cramping noggin

JOIN HERE ▶

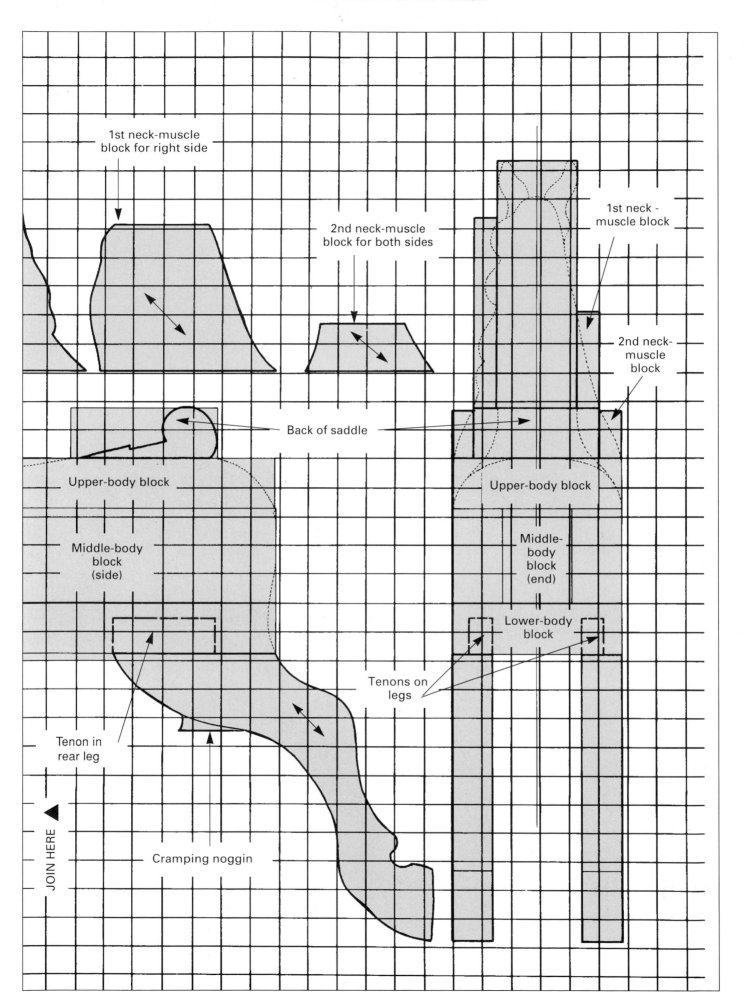

1st neck-muscle
block for right side

2nd neck-muscle
block for both sides

1st neck -
muscle block

2nd neck-
muscle
block

Back of saddle

Upper-body block

Upper-body block

Middle-body
block
(side)

Middle-
body
block
(end)

Lower-body
block

Tenons on
legs

Tenon in
rear leg

JOIN HERE

Cramping noggin

Plate 13.3 The right-hand side of the neck —
a little carving has already been started on the head

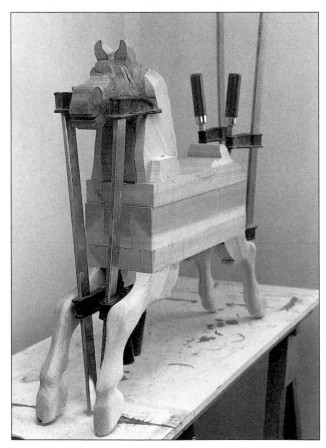

Plate 13.4 Showing how flats on the first neck-muscle
block aid cramping

mane (and the fancier carving) were done on the left side of the horse, which was the side on show. On European and American carousels, which go anti-clockwise, the right-hand side was more highly decorated. Since the horse we are making here is intended as a decorative arte-fact, not necessarily to be actually used on a merry-go-round, you can put the mane which-ever side you prefer.

Glue on the block for the back of the saddle. Plane the tops of the middle-body blocks flat, drill for four dowel pegs and glue down the upper-body block. That is all there is to the assembly. Pencil in the curve of the saddle and rump, and the outline of the scroll shape at the back of the saddle. With the horse on its side you can bandsaw off the waste along these pen-cil lines. But if your bandsaw has insufficient depth of cut, the waste will have to be chopped away with a large gouge and mallet. You will then have a profile which looks right in silhou-ette, but there are lots of corners to remove; the carving can commence.

CARVING

Carve off the corners of the neck-muscle blocks so that the neck tapers up from the shoulders, which are rounded over, but leave the mane proud. Turn upside down and shape the lower bulge of the chest between the front legs and

Plate 13.5 With all the blocks assembled the curve of the
rump and seat can be bandsawn (or carved) away

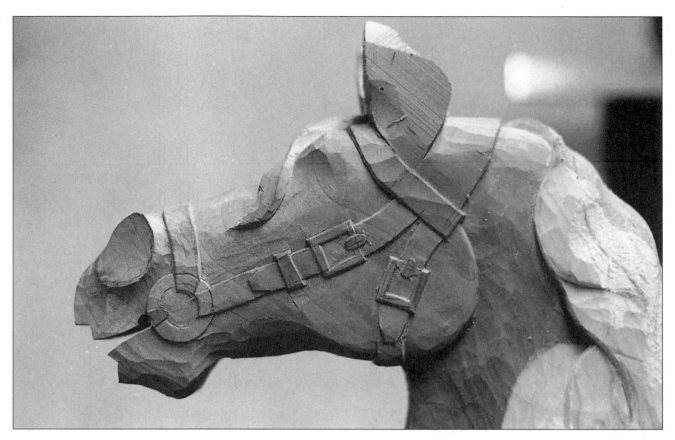

Plate 13.6 Try to ensure that the buckles stand proud of the straps, and the straps stand proud of the surrounding areas

the valley between the rear legs, and round and shape the legs, making the legs thinner above and below the knees. Round over the corners of the lower-body block. Turn it upright again and round over the saddle and the rump. The back of the saddle is shaped so that it curves smoothly into the back at each side. Pencil in the shapes of the ears — the waste between the ears can be cut away with a coping saw — and taper the head so that at the mouth it is no more than about 2in (51mm) wide, but leave the nostrils and the forelock proud.

Once you have removed the corners, and the shape begins to look more rounded and horse-like, pencil in some guidelines for the saddlery, breast plate and bridle, including the buckles. You can then cut along these lines with a straight chisel and carve back the wood on the waste side with a shallow gouge. The 'leather-work' needs to stand proud of the rest of the horse by $^1/_{16}$in-$^1/_8$in (2mm-3mm), more where two or three pieces of 'strap' overlap or cross. By the time you've finished, the tack should look as if it is on top of the horse, not carved into it. Careful and steady carving is needed to achieve the desired result. In the middle of the chest I carved a fancy round rosette, 2in (51mm) in diameter.

In addition to the six carving gouges listed in

Plate 13.7 The body has been rounded and rough sanded so you can make pencil guide marks for the saddlery

Chapter 2, I found I needed three more: a No 10 – $^1/_{16}$in (1.5mm) and a No 9 – $^1/_8$in (3mm) small, deep, straight London-pattern gouges, and a straight $^1/_4$in (6mm) 'V' tool. The small gouges are useful for picking out fine details in the carving and for making the buckle holes and horseshoe nails, and the 'V' tool is used to

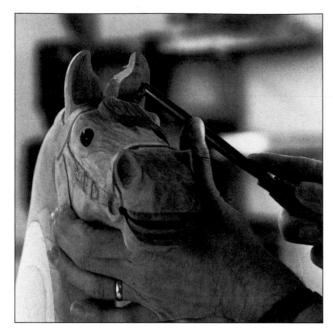

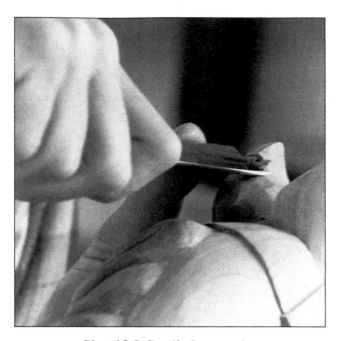

Plate 13.8 Hollowing the ears.
Note the glass eyes now in place

Plate 13.9 Detail of ear carving

make incised cuts along pencil guide lines such as the scroll at the back of the saddle, and for the hair. The mane and forelock are shaped to suggest a pleasing flow of hair, curling and interweaving, and the 'V' tool made cuts following the flow of the hair.

It is intended that Fig 2 showing the saddlery design on this horse, and the way the mane and forelock are made to curl and wave, should be

used as a guide only. You may like to refer to some of the many books dealing specifically with carousel-style horses (a few of which are listed in Appendix 3) for ideas on how these features, and indeed the overall shape and configuration of the horse, can be varied and enhanced. I have tried to keep this design as simple and straightforward as possible to make, whilst retaining the essential features of the

Plate 13.10 Progress is slow but steady

Plate 13.11 The carousel horse nears completion of the carving

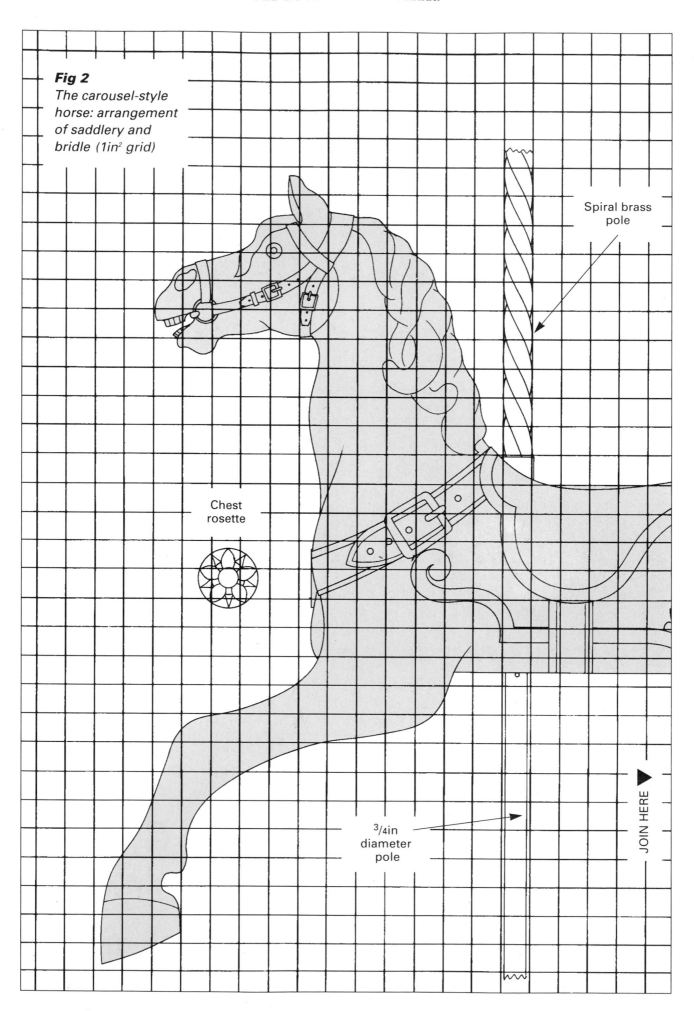

Fig 2
*The carousel-style
horse: arrangement
of saddlery and
bridle (1in² grid)*

Spiral brass
pole

Chest
rosette

³⁄₄in
diameter
pole

JOIN HERE ▶

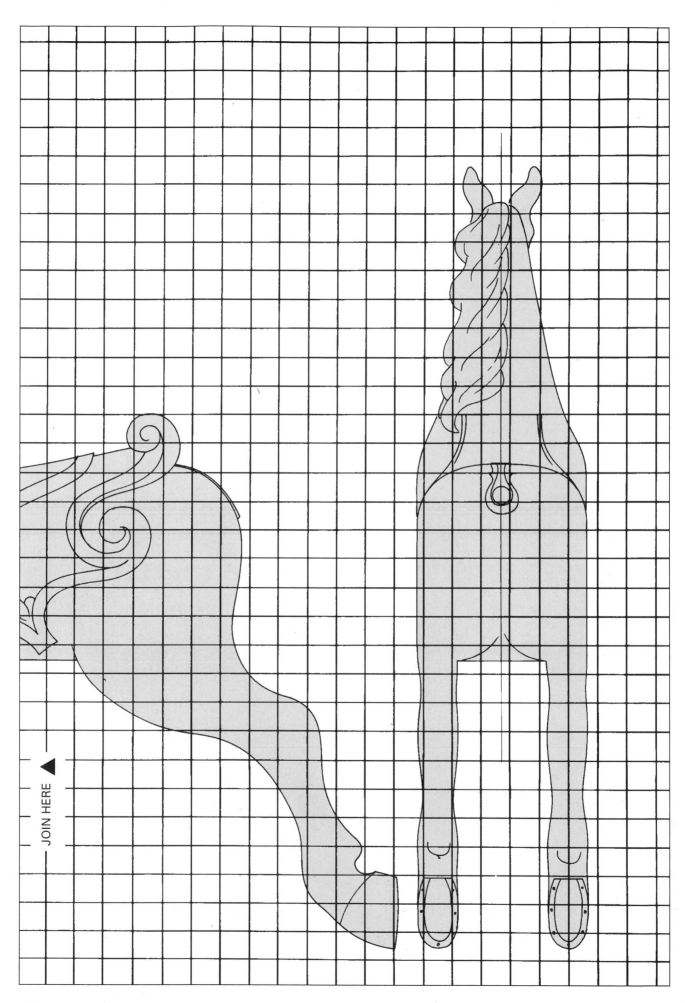

JOIN HERE ◄

Plate 13.12 Detail of carving on chest rosette

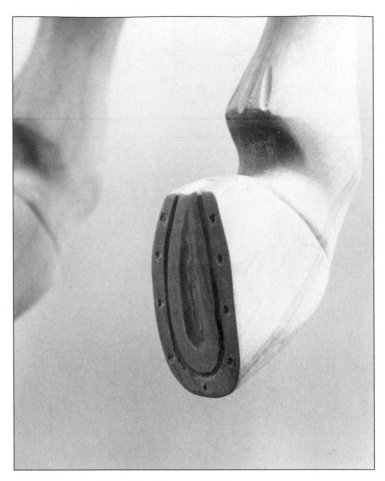

Plate 13.13 Detail of hoof

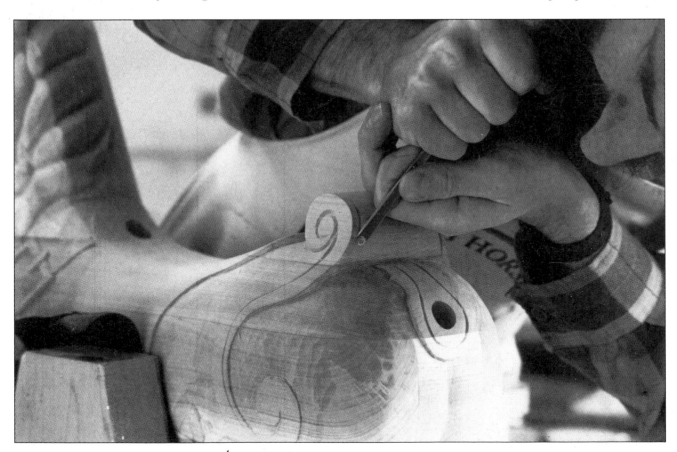

Plate 13.14 Using the V-tool to incise cuts on the saddle back

Plate 13.15 The white base coats give it a rather eerie look

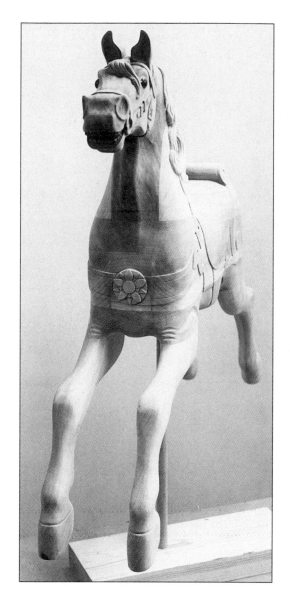 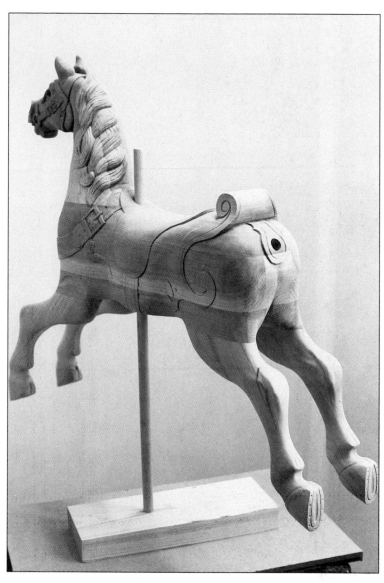

Plates 13.16–13.20 The carving, which is now complete, is shown here from various angles

carousel-style horse and remaining a fascinating woodworking project. The possibilities for variation are, as always, endless.

The tail hole is ¾in (19mm) diameter — note the bit of fancy carving around it, and is drilled right through to the hollow middle. The eyes are ⅝in (16mm) glass, set into recesses with woodfiller. The ears and nostrils are hollowed out a little, and the teeth defined with V-shaped cuts. It is important to keep your tools sharp, particularly when carving the mane and bridle, because these areas are difficult to sand off and clean cuts with your gouges will require very little sanding. In any case when sanding down, take care to keep your carving looking sharp and clean.

The pole on which the horse is mounted is a length of ¾in (19mm)-diameter ramin dowel (or metal pipe) 28in (710mm) long. Measure 11in (280mm) from the top end of the pole and here drill a small hole to take a 2in (50mm)-long steel pin on which the horse rests. I cut down a 4in (102mm) nail to make the pin. The lower end of the pole is inserted into a ¾in (19mm) hole drilled 1in (25mm) deep into a heavy block of timber 1¾in x 5¾in x 16in (45mm x 146mm x 406mm). You may wish to make up one rough base block and pole for mounting the horse on while you paint it, and then another, smarter one, for 'best'. The top of the dowel projects a few inches above the saddle and over this can be slotted a length of spiral brass tubing, to make the impression of a carousel horse complete.

FINISHING

I was tempted to leave my little carousel horse with a natural-wood finish, rather than cover all that careful carving with paint. But I then decided to give it a suitably bright colour scheme reminiscent of the highly varied colours used by traditional carousel artists. The painting was done with acrylics — first a coat of sanding sealer, then several of white primer undercoat rubbed down lightly between coats. The horse, excluding the saddlery and mane, was given an antique glaze (as described in Chapter 10), with added yellow paint, before painting in the colours. The horsehair tail, in this case mostly whitish hair with a bit of black hair added to echo the painting on the mane, was glued and wedged into its hole, and it is done. A delightful and decorative little horse that will enhance your home!

You might like to mount this horse on rockers. Although I have not designed it specifically with this in mind, and the design is unsuitable for mounting on a swing-iron stand (there being too little room between the legs for conventional swing irons), it is certainly possible to mount it on curved bow rockers. Fig 3 shows a very simple bow rocker arrangement suitable for this horse.

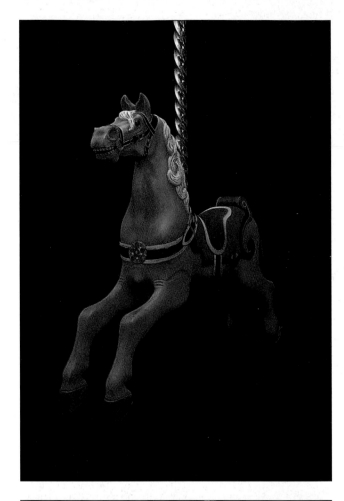

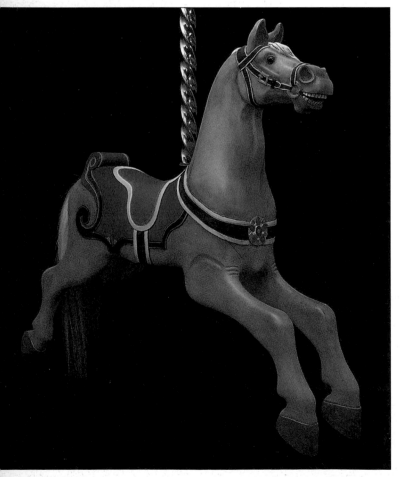

Plates 13.21–13.24 The finished carousel, complete with spiral brass pole

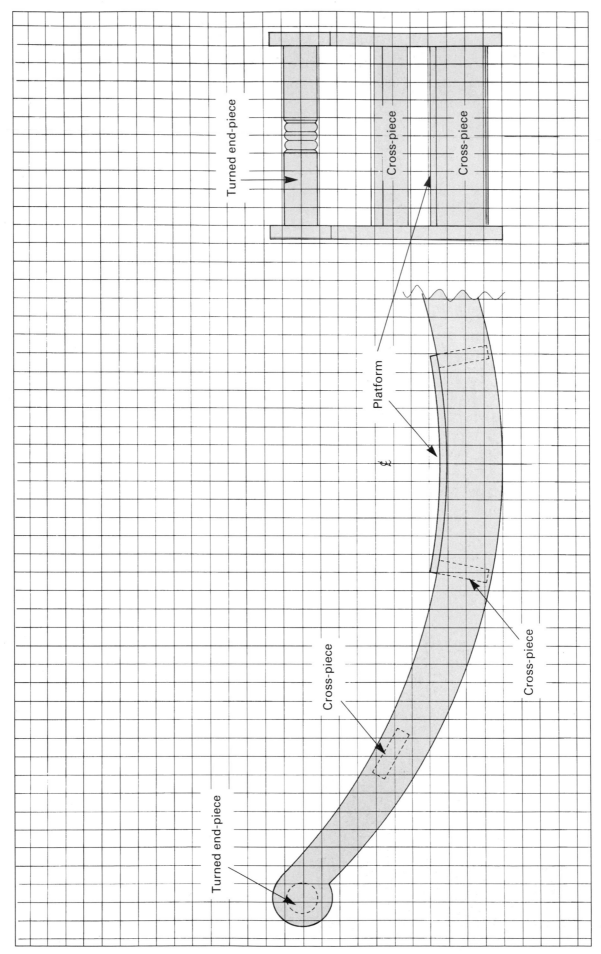

Fig 3 *Simple bow rockers for carousel-style horse (1in² grid)*

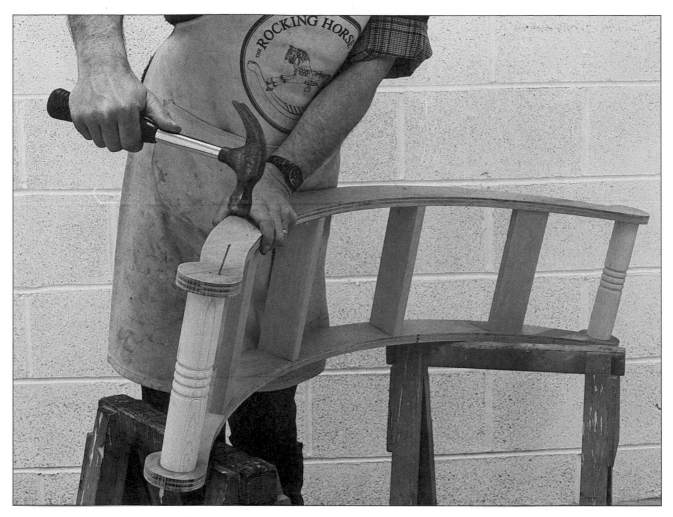

Plate 13.25 Making bow rockers for the carousel-style horse

*Plate 13.26 The finished carousel-style horse,
mounted on bow rockers*

The two rocker sides are parallel and connected together by cross-pieces, to which the horse's hooves are pegged, front and rear. Both rocker sides can be cut from a piece of ³⁄₄in (19mm) thick plywood 20in x 52in (508mm x 1321mm). They are glued and screwed onto the cross-pieces, which are all 10in (254mm) long, the end cross-pieces being 1³⁄₄in (45mm) square and turned, the rest ³⁄₄in x 2³⁄₄in (19mm x 70mm) and positioned as shown. The platform is ¹⁄₄in (6mm) thick plywood 11¹⁄₂in x 12in (292mm x 305mm) glued and pinned to the curved rocker sides. You may like to do a little shallow relief decorative carving to the rocker sides. It is then painted in acrylic colours that complement the horse and over-varnished.

CHAPTER 14
RESTORING OLD ROCKING-HORSES

Imagine a brand-new rocking-horse being taken from his maker's work-shop, paintwork gleaming bright and fresh, mane and tail long, clean and flowing, a sparkle in his glass eye. He is welcomed rapturously into a family and the young children take eager turns to ride. He is too big to be put away like other toys but stands quietly in the corner ever-ready for any interested child rider. Rocking to and fro, year in, year out, he grows old. His mane and tail are reduced to stubble. His once-fine harness deteriorates and breaks; the stuffing falls out of his saddle. An ear is chipped and broken. The continual rocking wears grooves in the steel bearers and he becomes rickety and unstable. The children outgrow him and he is put aside into a storeroom or shed.

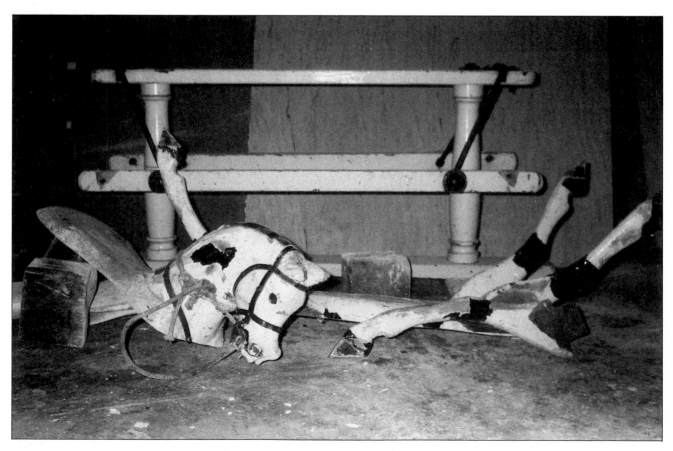

Plate 14.1 Long neglect in a damp shed equals a three-dimensional jigsaw puzzle

Plate 14.2 Fine early-nineteenth-century horse undergoing restoration

Years pass; the children grow up and a new generation of babies comes along. The old rocking-horse is remembered. He is brought out again and dusted off. But how small and sad and shabby he is! He is sent off to the restorer. There he is completely stripped down; his broken ear is repaired; he is patched up and repainted, just like of old. The rickety stand is attended to and cleaned and he is remounted. He is given a new harness, saddle, a new mane and tail. When the owners return to collect him

Plates 14.3/14.4 The same horse as in the previous photograph after restoration by the author

they can hardly recognise him, but beneath the bright new paintwork and trimmings survives the same old horse, now as good as new again, ready to begin a whole new life bringing continuing pleasure to countless children.

One evening a lady telephoned to ask if I would restore an old wooden rocking-horse. It had been hers when she was a child and she had kept it stored away against the advent of her own children. Now the time had come to bring Dobbin out again for her young son. 'He's very dirty,' she told me, 'but he is a lovely horse. I think he just needs a fresh coat of paint, and new mane and tail and saddle.'

When I went along to collect the rocking-horse I found Dobbin languishing behind a pile of old carpets and junk in a garden shed. I leaned over to lift him out and ... his head came off in my hand! 'I think,' I said slowly, 'that this will require more than a fresh coat of paint.'

Wooden rocking-horses can and do stand much abuse from children. (I once had one which appeared at first to have a terrible case of woodworm, until I realised it had been used as a target for darts' practice.) But they cannot stand damp conditions. Paint and gesso deteriorate

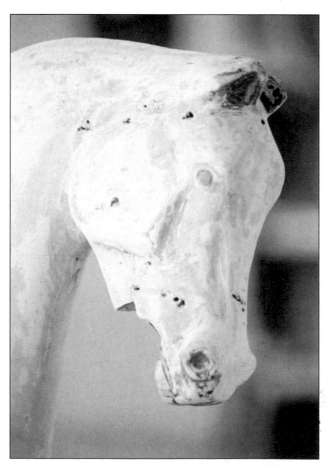

Plate 14.5 A well-worn old head. The lower jaw has broken off and the ears are badly damaged

and flake off, joints gape open, leather perishes. Many an old rocking-horse winds up in this sorry state, the combined ravages of use, abuse and neglect.

RENOVATE OR PATCH UP?

If you have or acquire an old rocking-horse apparently in need of renovation, how should you go about it? First, before you do anything else, carefully examine it, and try to determine exactly what sort of repairs and restoration it needs — if any. Take a number of photographs from various angles. There is a great temptation to start to strip off the old tack and paint straightaway, but desist from doing this until you feel quite sure that it really needs it. If your horse still has its original paintwork, albeit battered and chipped, you may be well advised not to attempt a full restoration at all. It is all too easy to spoil a rather nice, if dilapidated example of an old rocking-horse by inexpert attempts at repainting — I have done it myself (before I got better at it). And I often advise people to do the absolute minimum to an old rocking-horse, or nothing at all. Collectors, in particular, tend to prefer rocking-horses that retain their original paintwork and tack.

WOODWORM

Having said that, if your horse is really badly damaged and broken and if it has been poorly repainted in the past, then the best thing may well be to consider a complete renovation. The first thing to look for and treat, whether or not you have decided to undertake a complete renovation, is woodworm. Worm attack is most frequently found in the undersides of the stand or rockers, which were usually left unvarnished or unpainted. Sometimes it spreads up the posts and up into the legs. It is rarely found in the body or head where the paint has protected the wood. It should be treated with a proprietary woodworm killer squirted liberally into the holes. Usually, and if you are lucky, the worm infestation is not enough to affect the strength of the wood significantly and after treatment the wormy parts can be retained. But if the infestation is severe, to the point at which the wood is so riddled that it is disintegrating, the affected parts will need to be cut off and replaced.

REPAIRS

The horse can usually be quite easily taken off its stand or rockers by undoing the four hoof

Plate 14.6 Two old horses for restoration

Plate 14.7 Part of the private collection of J. and C. Carr in which every horse is in its original condition

Plate 14.8 Sawing off the damaged ears. Note the block that has been fixed on to rebuild the jaw

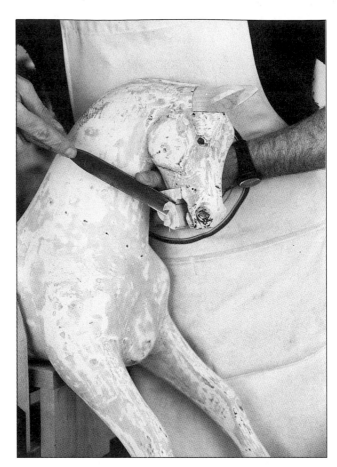

Plate 14.10 Carving the lower jaw

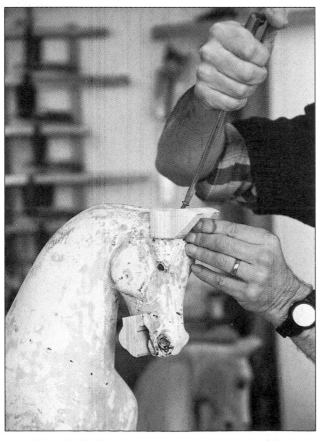

Plate 14.9 Fixing on a roughly bandsawn block for the new ears

Plate 14.11 Finishing off carving the new ears

bolts, though if corroded they may have to be hacksawn off. At this stage, give the horse a good shake to see if you can hear anything rattling about inside. It was not unusual for children to poke small objects into the horse either through its tail hole or through two pommel holes (of which more later) often found towards the front of the saddle. Over the years we have retrieved quite a collection of pens, cigarette cards, dice, hair pins and other small bric-a-brac from the insides of old horses. Sometimes these throw an interesting light on the history of the horse. Inside one rocking-horse which belonged to a school we found an old class list and managed to trace one of the names on the list. Now an elderly gentleman, he could remember quite clearly being allowed to ride the rocking-horse as a treat during his first week at school some seventy years before.

We have sometimes found pieces of newspaper used as padding under the saddle, which can help to date a rocking-horse — either when it was made, or previously restored. Often interesting aspects of a horse's history can be learned from its owner or past owners. The horse in plate 14.4 was originally made in 1805 for Lord Elgin. Its present owner, Mrs Fiona Hope, told us that it had been repainted in

Plate 14.12 This old horse is in original condition, but it is less likely to appeal to collectors of the finest rocking-horses

1911 to look like one of Queen Victoria's ponies, and it was to this sort of palomino colour that we were asked to restore it. Although in very battered condition when we received it, it is now back in everyday use as a plaything.

Chipped, crushed or broken ears are common. Slightly damaged ears can often be repaired by building up with woodfiller. Badly broken ears may need to be sawn off completely, replaced with new wood and re-carved. Although we try to retain as much of the original timber as possible, broken jaws or legs may also need to be replaced with new wood and re-

carved. Slight cracks in the woodwork, particularly along the joins, should not be too much of a problem and can be filled and sanded smooth. But if cracking is severe — if, for example, the horse has been stored in damp conditions and the old glue has disintegrated — then you may need to take the horse apart in order to re-fix the pieces together securely. I have on occasions rebuilt horses that have completely fallen to pieces. It is an interesting three-dimensional jig-saw puzzle and can involve more work than building a brand-new one. But if you can give a broken-down old

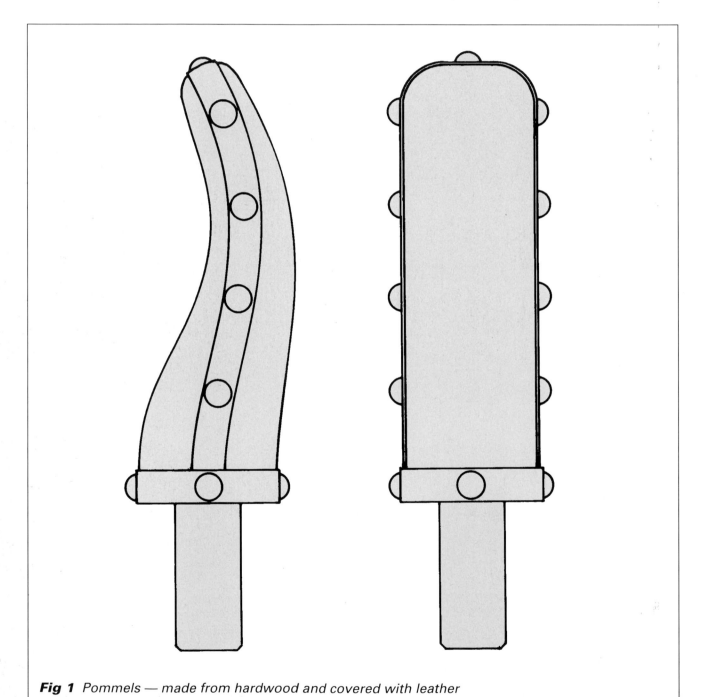

Fig 1 *Pommels — made from hardwood and covered with leather and decorated with small brass dome nails*

horse a new lease of life, then it is worth it. Would that we had access to such immortality.

With the woodwork repaired and sound, the remainder of the old paintwork can be removed. We prefer to use a hot-air paint stripper and scrapers for this, rather than chemical paint removers. Do not send the horse to be 'dipped and stripped' as this can seriously dam-

Plate 14.13 A fine old horse after restoration. Note the new buckle-on bridle and the pommels on the saddle

Plate 14.14 When a leg has broken right off it will have to be replaced

Plate 14.15 The tenon of the broken leg has been removed and a new leg bandsawn to shape with a new tenon

age your joints. Thoroughly sand smooth all over. There is no need to sand down to the bare wood unless the gesso has badly deteriorated, in which case you may have to think about re-gessoing (see Chapter 10). If the glass eyes are badly chipped or scratched, replace them; if they are good, keep them, but do take care not to scratch them when sanding down.

As mentioned earlier, on some old rocking-horses you will find two round holes in the horse (and in the original saddle if it survives), usually just above the stirrup staples. These were for the pegs of 'pommels' which were made of shaped hardwood covered in thin leather, with round pegs (see Fig 1). Their purpose was apparently to provide a secure seat for tiny children (who could hook their legs over them), or

to allow little girls to practise riding side-saddle. Since they were removable they are frequently lost and most restorers do not bother to replace them; they just fill (or leave) the holes, and fit the new saddle over them. However, new pommels can be fitted if you wish — you will need to cut round holes in the saddle flaps and/or skirts in the appropriate positions to align with the holes in the horse.

RENEWING TACK AND HAIR

The procedure for painting and tacking up the horse is as described in Chapters 10 and 11. Saddle shapes and styles do vary enormously but if you have the remains of the original saddle this can be copied. (See Appendix 2 for suppliers of accessories.) Some old horses have no saddle block but they can still be fitted with a nail-on type of saddle by fixing the back of the saddle tight down to the horse's back. Also, before nailing down the back of the saddle, tuck a length of strapping underneath the saddle top in the middle to form the tail strap or crupper. We tend to prefer to fit an old rocking-horse with a removable bridle — rather than the more common old practice of nailing on the bridle strapping — because it is nice for children to be able to remove the bridle in their play, and it saves having to hammer more nails into the old head.

Manes can be fitted into a groove cut in the horse's neck (as explained in Chapter 10), for which the neck should be prepared prior to painting. But most old horses were fitted with manes on hide, in other words a strip of hide with the hair still attached to it, and this type can still sometimes be obtained. The hide is simply nailed on down the horse's neck with 1in (25mm) wire nails. The nail heads are punched in and bury themselves out of sight in the hide.

STANDS AND ROCKERS

Stands and rockers were often originally varnished and the woodwork may only require a good clean and polish. Sometimes stands have painted stencils with the name of the original supplier and/or the patent date, and you should try not to obliterate these. A good preparation for cleaning dirty old varnish is a mixture of vinegar, white spirit and linseed oil, which will, when rubbed gently, remove dirt without damaging the old varnish. If the stand or rockers were originally painted — green seems to have been the favourite colour — they can either be cleaned, or stripped and varnished, or repainted if the underlying timber looks too rough to varnish. On stands, the swing irons and brackets will need to be removed, cleaned and probably repainted, and the bearing strips renewed if worn down.

Restoring old rocking-horses is a big subject, since there are so many different types and styles of horse, and so many problems that can arise, and it really deserves a whole book (see Bibliography). If you are in any doubt about how to tackle the restoration of an old rocking-horse, do seek professional advice.

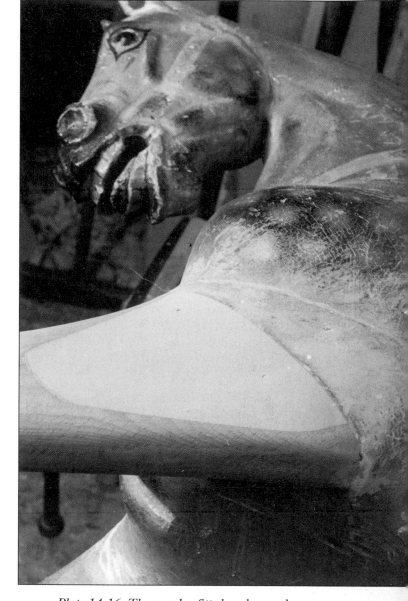

Plate 14.16 The new leg fitted and carved

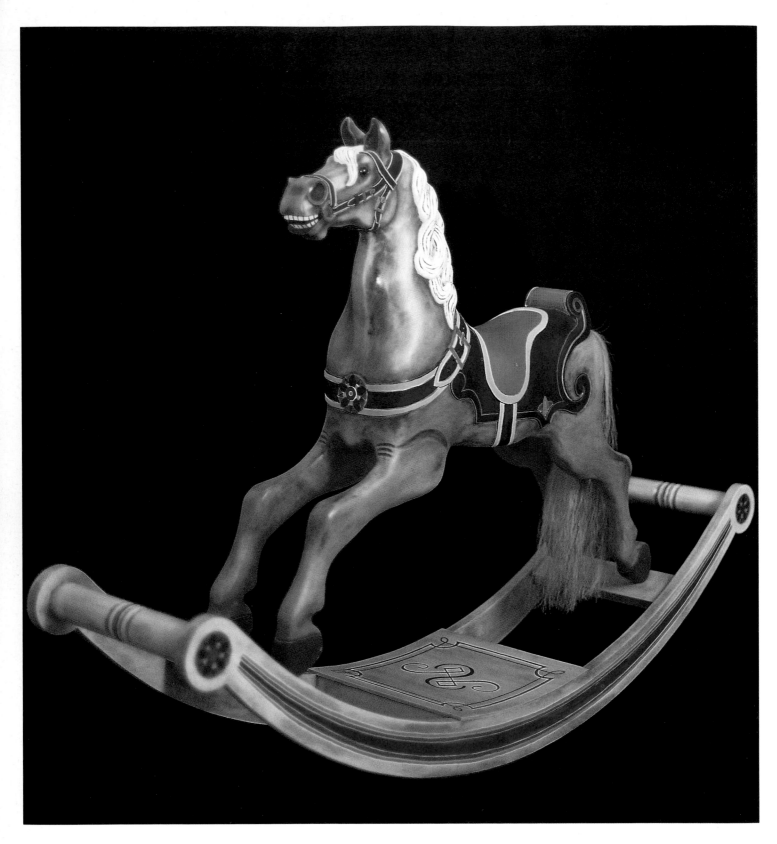

Carousel-style horse mounted on bow rockers

WOODWORKING TIPS

HOW TO SHARPEN WOODCARVING GOUGES

Keeping gouges sharp is vital for successful carving, and the softer the wood the sharper you need to keep them. Blunt gouges will tear at the fibres of the wood; sharp ones will cut cleanly through them, enabling you to work more quickly and effectively. How can you keep them razor sharp?

The conventional method is to use a slipstone — a small fine India or, preferably, Arkansas stone with rounded edges. The stone is oiled and a flat side is rubbed over the bevel of the tool until a fine burr of steel is formed on the inside, which is then removed using one of the rounded edges of the slipstone. There is quite a knack to doing this properly so that you get a gouge which is really sharp and evenly honed over the whole of the cutting edge. Even carvers of long experience sometimes have gouges whose cutting edge is of a distorted shape due to uneven honing, and it takes quite a bit of practice with the slipstone to get even a reasonably acceptable sharp edge. But there is a much easier method.

Fit a cotton polishing mop to one end of your grinder. Dress the mop with a steel cutting compound by holding the compound against the mop as it spins for a few seconds. Then hold your gouge so that the bevel rubs against the mop and, pressing gently, pivot the gouge so that every part of the bevel of the gouge has rubbed against the mop. A few seconds of rubbing is normally all that is necessary to achieve a

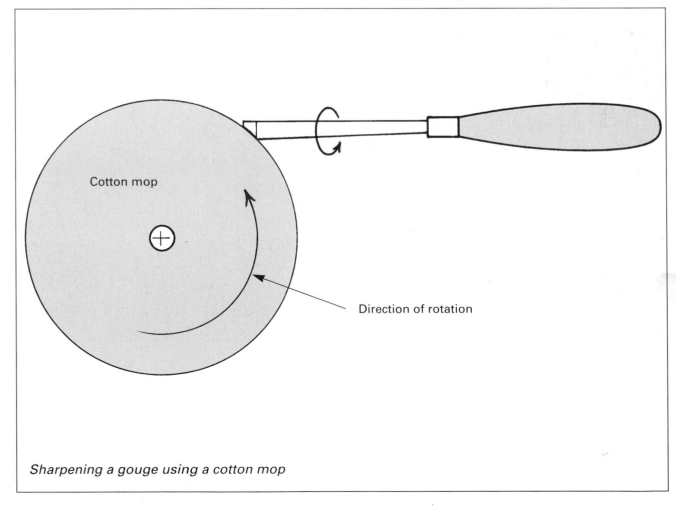

Cotton mop

Direction of rotation

Sharpening a gouge using a cotton mop

beautifully polished razor-sharp edge. With this method only a very minute quantity of steel is removed at each sharpening and the burr formed on the inside of the gouge is insignificant, so you do not need to bother trying to remove it. Also, your gouges will last much longer and need re-grinding far less frequently.

WARNING You must hold the gouge so that the cutting edge lies in the direction of rotation of the mop — do **NOT** hold the cutting edge up into the spinning mop as you would if it were a grinding wheel or it could dig in dangerously. Instead, reverse the direction of rotation (by turning the grinder round) so that the top of the mop is spinning away from you. You may need to move the grinder's tool rest out of the way, but **ALWAYS** wear eye protection.

For grinding, with a conventional stone wheel there is always the danger of the tool overheating. This does not happen if you use a hard rubber wheel. Again, have the top of the wheel turning away from you. Hold the gouge at right angles to the wheel and press the bevel gently against it, turning the gouge so that the whole of the bevel is evenly ground off. It will only take a few seconds and will leave the cutting edge evenly ground, ready to hone. Again, always wear eye protection.

THE USE OF DOWEL PEGS

There are two reasons for using fluted-dowel pegs in making a rocking-horse. First, they give extra strength to the joint. Second, since simple butt joints are used, the dowel pegs help to locate the two pieces being joined together, which would otherwise slide about while you are trying to cramp them up. Fluted-dowel pegs are used because the flutes allow excess adhesive to escape from the hole. The dowel holes should be slightly longer than half the length of the dowel peg used. A suitable dowel size for making a rocking-horse is $^5/_{16}$in diameter by $1^5/_8$in long (8mm x 40mm), and the drill bit should be the same diameter.

To ensure that the peg holes in the two pieces to be joined align exactly, use centre-point markers. Drill the holes in one piece to the required depth (use a twist drill with a screw-on depth guide to do this), and then place centre-point markers in the holes. Carefully put the other piece in place above the piece with the markers and press down firmly. The point of the markers will make a small mark exactly in line with the centres of the holes, which is where you drill the other hole(s). When glueing up dowelled joints, do not forget to put adhesive in both holes.

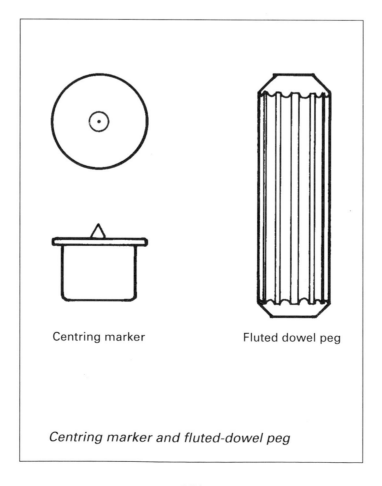

Centring marker   Fluted dowel peg

Centring marker and fluted-dowel peg

MAIL-ORDER SUPPLIERS OF TOOLS, ACCESSORIES AND FITTINGS

ENGLAND

The Rocking Horse Shop,
Fangfoss, York, YO4 5QH
Wide range of accessories and fittings (to fit all the designs in this book) for rocking-horse makers and restorers, full-size plans for rocking-horses and carver's chops, tools, timber packs, books and video. International mail-order service. (Send large self-addressed envelope and return postage for catalogue.)

Sue Austen Miniatures,
Folly End Farm, Ashton, Bishop's Waltham, Hampshire, SO3 1FQ
Twelfth-scale rocking-horse accessories and fittings.

John Boddy's Fine Wood and Tool Store,
Riverside Sawmills, Boroughbridge, North Yorkshire, YO5 9LJ
Timber, woodworking and carving tools, rocking-horse plans and accessories.

Craft Supplies,
The Mill, Millers Dale, Buxton, Derbyshire, SK17 8SN
Woodworking and carving tools, and rocking-horse plans.

W. Hobby Ltd,
Knights Hill Square, London SE27 OHH
Rocking-horse and other plans and accessories, modellers' tools.

The Model Shop,
44-46 Hounslow Road, Whitton, Middlesex, TW2 7EX
Sheet lime and other stripwood for miniature rocking-horses.

USA

Mike and Portia Mendenhall, Carousel Memories,
136 Old Orchard Drive, Los Gatos, California 95030
Rocking-horse and carousel plans and accessories.

AUSTRALIA

Hugh Galloway, U-Build Enterprises Ltd
PO Box 132, Rose Bay, Sydney 2029
Rocking-horse and other plans.

BIBLIOGRAPHY

Daiken, Lesley *Antique Toys and their Background* (Batsford, 1971)

Dew, Anthony *Making Rocking Horses* (David & Charles, 1984)

Fawdry, Marguerite *Rocking Horses* (Pollock's Toy Theatres, 1989)

Fraley, Maurice *Introduction to the Carousel* (Freels Foundation)

Fried, Frederick *A Pictorial History of the Carousel* (Barnes, 1964)

Green, Clive and Dew, Anthony *Restoring Rocking Horses* (Guild of Master Craftsman Publications, 1992)

Grober, Karl *Children's Toys of Bygone Days*

King, Constance *Antique Toys and Dolls* (Studio Vista/Christies, 1979)

Lambert, M. and Marx, E. *English Popular Art* (Batsford, 1951; reprint Merlin, 1989)

Manns, W., Shank, P. and Stevens, M. *Painted Ponies* (Zon International Publishing, 1987)

Mullins, Patricia *The Rocking Horse: A History of Moving Toy Horses* (New Cavendish Books, 1992)

Weedon, G. and Ward, R. *Fairground Art* (Abbeville Press, 1981)

White, Gwen *Antique Toys and their Background* (Batsford, 1971)

ACKNOWLEDGEMENTS

I would like to acknowledge the help given to me in preparing this book by the following people:

David Golledge of Holme upon Spalding Moor, who took most of the photographs, and whose advice on photography was invaluable.

Joe and Catherine Carr for permission to photograph their collection.

Norman Rowe for his photographs, and Dr Alan Robson for the loan of photographic equipment.

Sue Austen for her invaluable information and help in making the miniature twelfth-scale rocking-horse (and her photographs).

The staff at The Rocking Horse Shop: Phil Walsh, Barbara Brown, Josephine Marson, Barry Wood, Sue Rackham and Pauline Denham.

The Administrators of Nunnington Hall, North Yorkshire, and of The Sue Ryder Home, Holme upon Spalding Moor, who allowed us in with our photography equipment.

All those correspondents and visitors (too many to be named individually) who have offered advice, comment, information and criticism (which is always welcome and which I have tried to heed).

Pat Dew and our children, Sam, Kate and Lynn.

INDEX

INDEX